Law for Professionals

The *Law for Professionals* book series contains publications in all fields of the law aimed at professionals and practitioners. The book series is dedicated to publish high quality books that provide in-depth insights into the workings and the practical functioning of the law, international organizations or regional legal frameworks.

The authors contributing to the book series are experienced legal professionals and practitioners whose expertise combines theory and practice.

Madeleine Bernhardt

Leading Transformation in Law Firms

How Top Leaders Unlock Performance to Win the Future

Springer

Madeleine Bernhardt
DeepHumanScience
Berlin, Germany

ISSN 2662-141X ISSN 2662-1428 (electronic)
Law for Professionals
ISBN 978-3-031-98652-9 ISBN 978-3-031-98653-6 (eBook)
https://doi.org/10.1007/978-3-031-98653-6

This Springer imprint is published by the registered company Springer Nature Switzerland AG
The registered company address is: Gewerbestrasse 11, 6330 Cham, Switzerland

To all the leaders who courageously and passionately shape the future of the legal profession and lead the way—this book is for you.

Foreword

This time, it is for real. Market forces, regulatory developments, and, most importantly, the rise of artificial intelligence—technology unfathomable even 10 years ago—will be transforming the global legal profession in ways we are beginning to see but have little ability to predict. We are living in interesting times, paraphrasing the Chinese proverb, and we need to prepare.

Having spent over 19 years working in large law firms and 12 years teaching law firm and in-house leaders about the fundamentals of leadership, I am quite certain that corporate law firms are significantly underprepared to meet this moment. My deepest concerns center on fixed mindsets and a lack of leadership at the organizational, team, and individual levels across most legal organizations. Legal education around the world has neglected leadership as a discipline, and law firms have been able to rely upon traditional monopoly advantages and growing economies to generate wealth that no lawyers of my generation ever anticipated (or even desired, in many ways, but that's another story). With few exceptions, legal academics and the corporate law firms that subsidize legal education have dramatically underinvested in developing lawyers' leadership and professional skills, and their ability to build and leverage interdisciplinary problem-solving networks.[1]

Over the past 2 years, I have had the distinct pleasure of meeting and teaching with one of the rare exceptions in legal academia—Dr. Madeleine Bernhardt—who is at the forefront of helping law firms look to the future and rethink their business models and approaches to leadership. Leading Transformation in Law Firms is groundbreaking in so many ways—first and foremost because Dr. Bernhardt deeply cares about the people in the legal profession. With a background in business psychology as well as law, she is intensely curious about lawyers and delights in exploring the ways in which our inner psychology has shaped the way we organize, manage, and lead law firms. She has dedicated decades of scholarship to unlocking human potential for transformation in the legal profession, which in a human capital profession is truly the only effective place to begin. I was privileged to be one of the many people Dr. Bernhardt interviewed in connection with this book—privileged because in trading ideas and perspectives about law firms with her, I experienced first-hand her spark and passion for connecting dots and bridging the world of research and the real world of practice.

As a direct result of that spark and passion, this book brilliantly presents empirical, cutting-edge research about leadership and offers a bridge to law firm leaders: a clear, actionable framework—ACT-to-Transform®—to apply that research to transform their law firms at a time of great change and uncertainty. If you are a law firm leader, I strongly recommend that you read the book once through at a high level, noting the themes in the book that are most relevant to your firm's transfor-

1 See, e.g., Westfahl, Scott and Wilkins, David B., The Leadership Imperative: A Collaborative Approach to Professional Development in the Global Age of More for Less (August 3, 2017). *Stanford Law Review,* Vol. 69, No. 6, 2017.

mation journey and your own journey as a lawyer-leader. Then, as you encounter leadership challenges at the organizational, team, and/or individual leadership level, return to the book, easily locate the applicable chapter, and use the detailed, carefully crafted ACT-to-Transform® recommendations Dr. Bernhardt presents. You will have a roadmap to get started, and you'll be asking the right questions and thinking about the right issues to get going, which is often the hardest component of a transformation effort.

The need for strong legal institutions, including independent, thriving corporate law firms, could not be more important in these highly uncertain times. I am confident that Leading Transformation in Law Firms will help law firms become more adaptive to this moment and will help lawyer-leaders find their way forward more successfully, with more confidence, intentionality, and insight. Good luck on your journey and keep this book close at hand!

Scott Westfahl
Professor of Practice and Director
Harvard Law School Executive Education
Cambridge, MA, USA

Acknowledgments

I am deeply grateful to the many individuals who have supported, inspired, and contributed to this book in different ways.

First and foremost, I would like to thank **all the leaders whom I had the pleasure and privilege to interview for this book**. Their trust and openness in sharing their leadership experiences and challenges with me were essential to the development of the framework. Without their perspectives, stories, and insightful questions, I couldn't have written this book.

Thank you to each and every one of you (in alphabetical order):

- **Shruti Ajitsaria**, Partner and Head of Fuse, A&O Shearman
- **Zoë Andreae**, CEO, LECARE
- **Prof. Soledad Atienza, PhD**, Dean of IE Law School, IE University (Madrid)
- **Myriam Baars-Schilling**, Managing Partner, Oppenhoff
- **Moritz Berkenheide**, Head of HR, RSM Ebner Stolz
- **Luis de Carlos**, attorney at law, former Senior and Managing Partner Uría Menéndez, Chairman IE LawAhead Center on the Legal Profession
- **Javier Fontcuberta**, LL.M., Managing Partner Cuatrecasas
- **María González Gordon**, Co-Managing Partner, CMS Albiñana & Suárez de Lezo & Co-head of Digital Business Global Practice at CMS
- **Markus Hartung**, Founder of the Bucerius Center on the Legal Profession at Bucerius Law School and Managing Partner, Chevalier
- **Dr. Detlef Haß**, Managing Partner Germany, Hogan Lovells
- **Annette Höher-Bäuerle**, Managing Director and COO Germany, A&O Shearman
- **Prof. Dr. Klaus-Stefan Hohenstatt**, Partner People and Rewards, Freshfields
- **Laura Kind**, Global Head of Leadership, Learning and Organizational Development, Hogan Lovells
- **Elisabeth Lepique**, Managing Partner, Luther Rechtsanwaltsgesellschaft mbH
- **Dr. Matthias Lichtblau**, Director of Strategic Projects Europe & COO Germany, Dentons
- **Dr. Nadine Lilienthal**, Founder and CEO, LEGALEAP
- **Prof. Dr. Bruno Mascello, LL.M.**, EMBA HSG, attorney at law, Academic Director Law & Management, Executive School of Management, Technology and Law, University of St. Gallen
- **Prof. Moray McLaren**, Partner and Co-Founder LEXINGTON CONSULTANTS
- **Marc Ohrendorf, LL.M.**, International AI Management Board Chief of Staff at an international leading law firm, Director Bucerius Center on the Legal Profession
- **Prof. Dr. Wolfhart Pentz**, Director Leadership Advisory Germany, Egon Zehnder
- **Pedro Pérez-Llorca**, Senior Partner, Pérez-Llorca

- **Dr. Philipp Plog**, Managing Partner Germany, Fieldfisher
- **Dr. Tobias de Raet**, Partner and former Managing Partner, lindenpartners
- **Dr. Daniel Röder**, Partner and Founding Partner, Greenfort
- **Carlos Rueda**, Senior Partner, Gómez-Acebo y Pombo
- **Prof. Iñigo Sagardoy de Simón, PhD**, President, Sagardoy Abogados
- **Joan Roca Sagarra, LL.M.**, Executive Chair and Partner, RocaJunyent
- **Salvador Sánchez-Terán**, Managing Partner, Uría Menéndez
- **Dr. Stefan Sax**, Managing Partner Germany, Clifford Chance
- **Carsten Schneider, LL.M.**, Managing Partner Germany, Osborne Clarke
- **Prof. Dr. Michael Smets**, Professor of Management, Saïd Business School, University of Oxford
- **Andreas Steck**, Managing Partner Europe, Linklaters
- **Dr. Hariolf Wenzler**, CEO, YPOG and Director Bucerius Center on the Legal Profession
- **Scott A. Westfahl**, Professor of Practice and Director, Harvard Law School Executive Education
- **Karsten Wöckener**, Head of Germany, Partner, White & Case LLP.

I am tremendously grateful to my colleagues from the Bucerius Center on the Legal Profession—**Dr. Patrick Schroer, Julia Janoska, Dr. Hariolf Wenzler, Marc Ohrendorf, LL.M.**, and **Iris Wahl**. They were a constant source of inspiration and motivation throughout this endeavor, and I am extremely happy to collaborate with such an inspiring team.

I am deeply thankful to **Prof. Soledad Atienza**, Dean of IE Law School and Founder of the LawAhead Center on the Legal Profession, and to **Luis de Carlos**, former Senior and Managing Partner at Uría Menéndez and Chairman of the IE LawAhead Center. Not only did they readily agree to be interviewed and share their invaluable insights, but they were also extraordinarily generous in connecting me with Managing Partners from leading law firms in Spain—and in record time—which is nothing short of a miracle in a profession where time is such a scarce resource.

I am especially grateful to **Scott Westfahl**, Professor of Practice and Director of Harvard Law School Executive Education, for our wonderful collaboration, the incredibly insightful interview I had the pleasure of conducting with him, and the thought-provoking conversations we've shared. I am deeply grateful to him for so generously agreeing to write the Foreword to this book, especially given the extraordinary demands on his time.

I am also very grateful to **Dr. Bernhard Waltl**, Head of Legal Operations at the BMW Group and Co-CEO of the Liquid Legal Institute e.V. (LLI), **Kai Jacob**, Co-Founder of LDA GmbH & Co-CEO of the Liquid Legal Institute e.V. (LLI), and **Dr. Dierk Schindler, M.I.L.**, VP Legal, Mobility & Legal Innovation at Robert Bosch GmbH and Co-Founder of the Liquid Legal Institute e.V. (LLI), who were among the earliest supporters of this project. A heartfelt thank you as well to **Prof. Dr. Thomas Wegerich**, Co-CEO of the Federal Association of Commercial Law Firms in Germany (BWD e.V.) and Publisher at German Law Publishers GmbH, who supported this book from its very beginning.

I am very grateful to **Dr. Matthias Lichtblau**, Director of Strategic Projects Europe & COO Germany at Dentons, and to **Dr. Hariolf Wenzler**, CEO at YPOG and Director of the Bucerius Center on the Legal Profession, for their valuable input on the interview questions and their insightful feedback at various stages. I would also like to thank **Dr. Alexander Insam, M.A.**, lawyer and partner at GÖRG, for the inspiring exchange we had very early on in this project.

This book would not have been possible without the highly professional and dedicated support of **Manuela Schwietzer**, Associate Editor at Springer, and **Julia Bieler**, Senior Editorial Assistant, at Springer. Their thoughtful coordination, responsiveness, and flexibility were invaluable throughout the entire process.

I would also like to thank **Tobias Heumann** for creating the chapter-opening illustrations and Figs. 1.1, 2.1, and 6.1, and **Stephan Katz** for creating Fig. 4.2.

My heartfelt thanks go to **my family and friends** for their constant encouragement, their interest and curiosity, and for cheering me on at every stage of the journey.

Last—and truly first—I would like to thank my husband, **Andreas Bernhardt**, for being the kindest reader and most constructive critic of each chapter, for his unwavering support, his ability to always put things into perspective, and his incredible sense of humor.

Contents

About the Author

Prof. Dr. Madeleine Bernhardt, LL.M. is a leading expert on the future of leadership in the legal profession. She is the founder of Deep Human Science, a leadership advisory in Berlin, and serves as Director of the Bucerius Center on the Legal Profession (CLP) at Bucerius Law School in Hamburg. With a unique dual background in law and psychology, she helps law firm leaders and senior executives master transformation by unlocking human performance across the firm. Her keynotes, advisory work, and research focus on how leaders build future-ready, adaptive organizations and lead with psychological intelligence in times of disruption.

Alongside her work with professional services firms, Madeleine advises lawyers in international arbitration on managing complex psychological dynamics, and supports leaders in police organizations in navigating high-stakes leadership challenges. She studied law in Cologne and Paris I (Panthéon-Sorbonne), holds a doctorate in law, and is a qualified psychologist with a Master's degree from the Free University of Berlin.

Introduction

Contents

M. Bernhardt, *Leading Transformation in Law Firms*, Law for Professionals,
https://doi.org/10.1007/978-3-031-98653-6_1

> It is not the strongest of the species that survives, nor the most intelligent that survives. It is the one that is the most adaptable to change.[1]—Charles Darwin

You are leading your firm at a defining moment. Rapid technological advancements, increasing competition, sometimes from highly unexpected places, evolving client demands, and shifting workforce expectations are reshaping the legal landscape right before your eyes. Every firm, including yours, is feeling the impact.

At times like this, significant change is a given, but long-term success is not.

To stay ahead of your competitors, you need to build a future-ready firm—one that successfully responds to disruptive developments and proactively drives transformation across the organization. Darwin's observation is still true: adaptability drives survival. Your firm's long-term success and growth require a strategy that strengthens your firm's adaptive capacity to evolve at speed. Your success will depend on how effectively you lead that shift.

If you embrace transformation as a continuous priority, your firm will not just survive; it will thrive. If you don't, others will. And likely, they will leave you behind.

After all, in today's legal market, the firms that succeed are the ones that can *"continuously transform at speed."*[2]

Transformation: More than Change

Transformation goes beyond change in both depth and complexity.

Organizational transformation *"is the comprehensive process of realigning your business's structure, culture, and operations to adapt to internal or external changes."*[3]

While *"change"* typically focuses on a few discrete and defined shifts, transformation *"is much more unpredictable, iterative, experimental and entails much higher risk."*[4] It involves multiple interdependent activities, such as discovering a new or revised business model and reinventing the organization to succeed in the future. Whether triggered by significant external or internal forces, transformation reshapes the very foundation of your firm.

For your firm's transformation to succeed, you as a leader will need to proactively anticipate future demands and courageously challenge and adapt existing structures, processes, beliefs, and habits.

You will also need to initiate profound shifts in behaviors, mindsets, decision-making processes, and roles—at every level of the firm. Moreover, at its core, transformation ultimately challenges the very identity of your organization, forcing you to answer the question: *"What value does your firm provide, and how do you deliver it?"*

---

1 Darwin (1859).
2 Gardner and Fealy (2022).
3 Einstein (2025).
4 Korova (2021), p. 7.

The Human Factor: Why Transformation Succeeds—or Fails

You are undergoing transformation to build a future-ready firm, strategically driving growth, adapting quickly to external shifts, and driving necessary change across your firm.

But transformation success is far from guaranteed.

For three decades, research has consistently shown that many transformations fail. In 1995, Harvard Business School professor John Kotter found that **about 70% of organizational transformations did not succeed**. A recent EY and Oxford study[5] revealed similar results: In a survey of over 900 C-suite executives, **67% of leaders said they had experienced at least one underperforming transformation** in the last 5 years.

This brings us to the big question:

? Why do so many transformations fall short?

Of the approximately 70% of transformations that fail, only about **25%** are due to structural or budgetary challenges. A staggering **75%** of outcomes hinge on the human factor.

Ultimately, transformation success—or failure—comes down to people. The EY and Oxford study authors concluded that the "*key to turning transformation failure into success relies on the ability of organizations and their leaders to completely redesign transformations with humans at the center.*"[6]

Having a strong focus on human potential and performance is crucial to your firm's success, both in responding to external shifts and driving internal transformations. It enables you to

- attract, develop, and retain top talent
- unlock peak performance in individuals and teams, helping them reach their full potential
- leverage multidisciplinary collaboration to deliver greater value to clients
- build a strong, adaptive culture that responds quickly to disruption and fosters innovation.

Moreover, leading with a strong focus on human performance is directly linked to business outcomes: Firms that strongly focus on enabling people and teams to successfully transform *"are **2.6 times** more likely to be successful than those that do not"*—with a **73% chance of success versus only 28%.**[7]

Leading transformation requires leadership skills far beyond "leading change".

While change often involves guiding people through isolated, incremental adjustments, such as adopting new technologies or refining workflows, leading transformation is far more complex.

5 White et al. (2023).
6 Saïd Business School & EY (2022).
7 Saïd Business School & EY (2022), p. 12.

You must lead people, teams, and yourself through a fundamental shift in how the firm operates, collaborates, and delivers value.

While change fits within existing structures, transformation challenges deep-seated assumptions, reshapes the firm's identity, and requires a culture shift. People must unlearn ingrained habits, redefine their roles, embrace uncertainty, and commit to a different future, all of which create significant emotional and cognitive strain.

This is why transformations stall—not due to poor strategy, but because leaders underestimate the human complexities involved.

Successful transformation leaders build trust, foster psychological safety, and inspire people to think and act differently. They lead through ambiguity, sustain momentum amid resistance, and create a culture of adaptability, ensuring that transformation is not just implemented but truly embraced.

Unlocking Peak Performance During Transformation

For a long time, I have been fascinated by human behavior in organizations. Questions like, *"What determines how effectively people adapt when their organization undergoes significant change?" and "What kind of organizational environment is needed for people and teams to truly perform and thrive?"* have driven my curiosity.

Given this interest, it was only natural that, in addition to my background in law, I specialized in business psychology.

Since then, I have spent nearly two decades working closely with leaders in national and international law firms to enhance their leadership effectiveness. Through this work, I have witnessed firsthand the profound impact of leadership on an organization's culture, motivation, and performance, and, by extension, on a firm's ability to adapt and remain competitive.

Historically, many law firms have been highly successful and have seen little need for transformation. Business was thriving, and, in many cases, still is. Even as legal tech evolved, discussions around adaptability and speed of change remained somewhat peripheral. Innovations such as automation and the streamlining of routine tasks, while valuable, did not appear disruptive enough to necessitate immediate action.

However, the emergence of generative artificial intelligence (AI) has changed this dynamic. The conversation is no longer about incremental efficiency gains; it is about how law firms will address **change at the very core of legal work**.

A recent white paper by Simon-Kucher & Partners (2025)[8], in collaboration with the Bucerius Center on the Legal Profession, explores how generative AI will disrupt the traditional commercial model of law firms.

8 Simon-Kucher & Partners in collaboration with Bucerius Center on the Legal Profession (2025).

The authors predict that law firms must gradually *"adopt a plurality of business and commercial models"*[9]—expanding beyond the traditional commercial model to include software-driven business structures.

Moreover, they anticipate a **profound shift in law firm culture**. Future law firms are expected to operate more like corporations, with a clearer division of labor, increased centralization in decision-making, and more sophisticated approaches to market strategy and revenue generation. A major cultural challenge will be the need for leaders to share authority and embrace collaboration—not only among lawyers but also with professionals from other disciplines. The authors emphasize that this shift is not just difficult but essential:

"This cultural change is seen as the number one challenge by Managing Partners, ranking well ahead of technical obstacles or imperfections in the technology itself."[10]

With law firms facing such fundamental shifts, I began focusing more on leading transformation as a key challenge. In particular, I asked the question:

? How can you unlock people's untapped potential to drive transformation and secure your firm's future-readiness?

I have examined this question from every angle:

- Building on insights from my earlier **research**, *"The Future of Leadership"*, conducted by the Bucerius Center on the Legal Profession in partnership with Egon Zehnder[11], I delved into 30 years of research on the **success factors of transformation**.
- For this book, I also conducted **35 interviews—with Managing Partners, CEOs, and COOs from leading law firms**, as well as top leadership scholars from internationally renowned business and law schools.
- Drawing on these interviews, extensive research, my professional background in law and psychology, and over 20 years of experience in the legal industry, I developed a holistic framework, the ACT-to-Transform® Framework.

i The ACT-to-Transform® Framework covers **nine critical areas** that leaders should focus on to unlock human potential and drive peak organizational performance during transformation.

Each area helps you shape a future-ready firm—one that has a strong culture and adapts quickly in a competitive environment. Together, they enable you to implement your firm's strategy, including necessary transformations across the entire organization, by unlocking human performance. They help you build a fast-

9 Simon-Kucher & Partners in collaboration with Bucerius Center on the Legal Profession (2025), p. 24.

10 Simon-Kucher & Partners in collaboration with Bucerius Center on the Legal Profession (2025), p. 14 [emphasis added].

11 Bucerius Law School Center on the Legal Profession & Egon Zehnder (2021).

1

Fig. 1.1 The ACT-to-Transform® Framework: Unlocking human performance for a future-ready firm

learning, adaptive firm, which is *"the critical success factor during periods of transformation and systemic change."* [12]

Following the ACT-to-Transform® Framework will help you secure your firm's long-term success by empowering individuals and teams to seize opportunities for development and growth, reinvent how they work and collaborate, and perform at their best amid constant change.

You will build a *"radically human organization"*[13]—one *"that creates space for people to grow, change, and reach more of their full potential."*[14].

Figure 1.1 highlights the critical areas that come together in the ACT-to-Transform® Framework.

---

12 Brassey et al. (2021).
13 KORN FERRY (2021).
14 Cooks-Campbell (2022).

What to Expect from This Book

The ACT-to-Transform® Framework will serve as your guide throughout the book. Here's what you can expect as you move through this book to unlock transformational change in your organization.

Three Levels to Watch

The book is structured across three levels—individual, team, and organization. One of the things that makes leading through transformation so challenging is that you need to **skillfully switch between these three interrelated levels continuously**.

Part I (► Chaps. 2, 3, 4) focuses on the **organizational level** and enables you to shape your organization's strategic and cultural capacity to transform your firm.

Part II (► Chaps. 5, 6, 7) zooms in on **teams** and explores how you can foster your team's capacity to handle and drive transformation.

Part III (► Chaps. 8, 9, 10) focuses on supporting **individuals** in successfully transforming mindsets and behaviors to skillfully handle transformation and thrive amidst challenges.

What might this look like in practice?

Learning from leaders in different industries with similar challenges who have successfully transformed their organization through skillfully moving across the three levels can be useful.

Take, for example, Microsoft's radical culture transformation toward a *"Growth Mindset"* across the whole company. Microsoft was experiencing serious threats from mobile devices, cloud computing, and the rise of Google and Amazon[15] when Satya Nadella became CEO in 2014. Along with his Chief People Officer, Kathleen Hogan, Nadella successfully led Microsoft's digital transformation, shifting Microsoft's focus towards cloud technology, transforming the company culture toward employee empowerment, and turning the company around.

Nadella skillfully utilized several key areas from the ACT-to-Transform® Framework by analyzing the company thoroughly using systems thinking, transforming the company's culture to change the business model (**organizational level**), and embarking on a 9-month *"listening tour"*, where he actively engaged people and teams (**team level**) in defining key elements of a new culture. These efforts culminated in a meeting of the 180 Corporate Vice Presidents, where each individual committed to a "Growth Mindset" (**individual level**)—a key factor for effective continuous learning across the company. Leveraging the interrelated key areas of the ACT-to-Transform® Framework skillfully allowed Nadella to transform it into an undisputed market leader in a fiercely competitive environment.

15 O'Reilly (2024), p. 42.

Nine Focus Areas to Empower Human Performance
In each chapter, one of the nine key areas is in the spotlight. In each chapter, you get actionable insights on a key area where it's crucial for you to fully leverage human potential in a way that benefits individuals, teams, the firm and, of course, the clients you serve.

Three Steps to Follow: The ACT Process
In each chapter, you will explore the provided tools with a simple three-step process to drive human performance:

Step 1: Acknowledge the current status and leverage diagnostic tools to uncover barriers and opportunities at the individual, team, and organizational levels.

Step 2: Challenge previously unquestioned assumptions, behavioral patterns and systems that don't serve your firm's transformation goals. This will require you to ask tough questions, encourage experimentation, and disrupt old patterns that hold your firm back.

Step 3: Transform assumptions, behavioral patterns, and systems using targeted tools and techniques to embed transformation into the fabric of your firm.

Using Insights to Help Clients Unlock Human Performance

Your clients face their own transformation challenges, from external pressures to completely rethinking how they operate in a fast-changing world. Your job is to understand what these challenges are and how your firm can help solve them.

The more your people and teams skillfully apply the tools and insights from the ACT-to-Transform® Framework, the better they will understand your clients' respective challenges.

As a result, your people will become more adept at offering value through insightful questions and impulses that spark new perspectives in clients. This will ultimately help your clients drive transformation by unlocking human performance in their organizations. In doing so, your people and teams will deepen their role as trusted advisors, transcending the legal arena to embrace a more holistic focus on your clients' systems.

Who This Book Is for and What You Will Gain

In a word, this book is for leaders. Whether you are a Managing Partner, CEO, COO, CHRO, CTO, CIO, business services leader, or a team leader within your firm—or even if you hold no formal leadership title but are passionate about increasing your positive impact—this book is for you.

More specifically, this book is for leaders who:

- are committed to building their firm's long-term success by driving strategic growth in an increasingly complex and competitive landscape
- aim to shape a future-ready firm—one that adapts quickly to external shifts and internal changes to deliver maximum value to clients
- strive to transform their firm successfully and sustainably.

As you read this book, you will learn how to unlock human potential in a way that benefits your firm, your clients, your people and teams, and yourself. By the end of the book, you will have gained:

- practical tools and actionable insights to grow your firm's human and psychological capital to shape a firm that thrives in disruptive times
- new approaches to creating a culture of sustainable growth powered by trust and continuous shared learning
- strategies to inspire, empower, and enable individuals and teams to adapt quickly, collaborate effectively, and perform at their best
- insights that help you deliver outstanding client experiences by fully leveraging your firm's collective potential.

Reflection and Action: Twin Engines for Successfully Leading Transformation

» We do not learn from experience… we learn from reflecting on experience.—John Dewey

Throughout this book, you will encounter impulses designed to help you reflect on your current challenges and consider how to apply what you read to your own reality. I know from my own experience that such exercises are often skipped because they require effort and a little time.

However, as Dewey rightly points out, when we neglect reflection, we block our ability to learn. In nearly every interview I conducted with senior leaders, one theme stood out: the lack of time for systematic reflection, particularly when it comes to effective leadership. Most leaders are caught in "firefighting mode," constantly managing crises that leave little room for strategic thinking or long-term planning. This relentless pace not only stifles reflection but also hinders personal and professional growth.

? How will you make time for reflection and action?

Make a plan now to ensure you get the most out of this book and its exercises. **Now, let's go and grow.**

References

Brassey, J., De Smet, A., Kothari, A., Lavoie, J., Mugayar-Baldocchi, M., & Zolley, S. (2021, August 2). Future proof. Solving the 'adaptability paradox' for the long term. *McKinsey & Company*. https://www.mckinsey.com/capabilities/people-and-organizational-performance/our-insights/future-proof-solving-the-adaptability-paradox-for-the-long-term

Bucerius Law School Center on the Legal Profession & Egon Zehnder. (2021). *The future of leadership*. https://www.law-school.de/fileadmin/content/law-school.de/de/units/abt_education/Studienseite/Studien/CLP_2022_Future_Download.pdf

Cooks-Campbell, A. (2022, January 20). Becoming more you: What it means to transform as a human. *BetterUp*. https://www.betterup.com/blog/human-transformation

Darwin, C. (1859). *On the origin of species by means of natural selection, or the preservation of favoured races in the struggle for life*. John Murray. Retrieved February 12, 2025, from https://darwin-online.org.uk/content/frameset?itemID=F373&viewtype=text&pageseq=1

Einstein, B. (2025, January 21). Leading successful organizational transformation through culture. *Harvard Business School Online*. https://online.hbs.edu/blog/post/organizational-transformation

Gardner, E., & Fealy, L. (2022, October 20). How transformations with humans at the center can double your success. *EY*. https://www.ey.com/en_gl/insights/consulting/how-transformations-with-humans-at-the-center-can-double-your-success

KORN FERRY. (2021, July 6). The future of organizations is here. The future is radically human. *KORN FERRY*. https://www.kornferry.com/content/dam/kornferry-v2/featured-topics/pdf/the-future-is-radically-human.pdf

Korova, I. O. (2021). Research of transformation models leading to organizational performance improvement. *IOSR Journal of Business and Management, 23*(12), 7–20. https://doi.org/10.9790/487X-2312020720

O'Reilly, C. (2024). How Microsoft transformed its culture: Five levers for organizational cultural change. *Management and Business Review, 4*(1), 41–50. https://doi.org/10.1177/2694105820240401006

Saïd Business School & EY. (2022). *The future of transformation is human*. University of Oxford. https://www.sbs.ox.ac.uk/sites/default/files/2024-04/ey-the-future-of-transformation-is-human-report.pdf

Simon-Kucher & Partners in collaboration with Bucerius Center on the Legal Profession. (2025). The AI-Conomics of legal services. How generative AI will transform the commercial model of law.

White, A., Wheelock, M., Canwell, A., & Smets, M. (2023, May 10). 6 key levers of a successful organizational transformation. *Harvard Business Review*. https://hbr.org/2023/05/6-key-levers-of-a-successful-organizational-transformation

Organizational Level

Contents

Apply Systems Thinking to Align Strategy and Execution

Contents

M. Bernhardt, *Leading Transformation in Law Firms*, Law for Professionals,
https://doi.org/10.1007/978-3-031-98653-6_2

» A bad system will beat a good person every time.—William Edwards Deming[1]

For years, the full-service, mid-sized Bristol-based law firm VWV thrived on its reputation, legal expertise, and strong client relationships. Then, the external environment shifted dramatically. The rise of artificial intelligence and automation began reshaping the legal profession. Former Law Society president Christina Blacklaws warned that British law firms risked *"losing"* their *"place in the world"* if they did not embrace technology *"harder and faster"*.[2]

VWV's leadership saw the risk: without action, they faced declining competitiveness and potential client losses. The firm's leadership decided they needed a fundamental strategic transformation to incorporate AI into their operations.

VWV set out with a clear **vision**: to become a leader in AI-driven legal services, enhancing efficiency while maintaining legal excellence. They decided to make *"strategic investments in technology and digital capabilities to enhance its service offerings and client experience"*,[3] providing faster, smarter, and cost-effective client solutions. They embedded AI into their broader **innovation and digital strategy**,[4] and ensured its execution by aligning all **internal operations**.

In particular, they focused on the following key components:

▪ Structure and Metrics

VWV's Managing Partner, Steven McGuigan, and Director of Digital, Data & Technology, Dave Bloor, came up with the idea for an *"AI innovation programme"* that would position junior lawyers at the core of the firm's innovation efforts, shaping the firm's AI strategy. They formed a strategic partnership with the legal technology company *Robin AI* to develop customized AI solutions across the entire firm, and VWV became "*the first law firm in the world*"[5] to launch such a comprehensive AI training with trainees as front and center of the firm's innovation strategy.

▪ Tasks

VWV redefined its core tasks by incorporating AI into routine legal work. They utilized AI tools to automate document analysis, contract review, and legal research, significantly reducing the time required for these tasks and allowing lawyers to focus on more complex, value-added activities. In collaboration with the legal tech company Robin AI, the firm streamlined contract review processes by 80%.[6]

1 Deming (1993).
2 Baksi (2025).
3 McCann (2024).
4 For more details, please refer to McCann (2024).
5 Robin AI (n.d.).
6 Williams (2023).

- **People**

Within 6 months, junior lawyers identified over 50 challenges where AI could optimize legal services and pitched their ideas directly to firm leadership.[7] Dave Bloor, VWV Director of Digital, Data &Technology, emphasized: *"Having our freshest minds re-thinking how AI can change the delivery of legal services helps define our lawyers of the future."*[8]

- **Culture**

AI adoption was initially met with internal skepticism. Some partners were unsure whether inexperienced junior lawyers would be able to identify problems that could be solved by using AI, while others feared that AI-driven processes could undermine their expertise, judgement, and reputation among clients who expected high-touch, bespoke legal services. VWV addressed these concerns directly. As Managing Partner McGuigan emphasized, *"trainees bring fresh perspectives on how AI can enhance, rather than replace, the human elements of legal practice … incorporating AI while maintaining the highest standards of legal excellence."*[9]

VWV fostered a **culture of innovation** by empowering trainees to identify problems that could be solved with AI and involving them in developing AI-based legal solutions, engagement and confidence increased.[10] This bottom-up approach to innovation fostered a "growth mindset" (see ▶ **Chap.** 8) across the firm which is essential for a culture of innovation.

The firm's strategic approach paid off:
- VWV strongly increased efficiency. AI-driven tools helped cut time spent on drafting reports and analyzing contracts by over 50%, giving lawyers more time for strategic client work.[11]
- Lawyers across the firm are increasingly engaged in using AI. Younger lawyers are highly committed to the firm, feeling they are able to make a meaningful contribution. The *"AI innovation programme"* will be repeated, and McGuigan expects it to attract top talents who are being offered to develop future skills.
- VWV generated £54.2 million in revenue during the 2023–2024 fiscal year and anticipates a 13% increase, bringing it to £61 million in the following fiscal year. The firm views the effective integration of AI and other technologies as a crucial factor in achieving its target turnover of £95 million within the next 5 years.[12]

VWV displayed the execution of key success factors in organizational transformation:
- proactively assessing shifts in the external environment that can impact the firm's performance

7 Ackerman (2025) and Hilborne (2024).
8 Robin AI (n.d.).
9 Robin AI (n.d.).
10 Hilborne (2024).
11 Ackerman (2025).
12 Ackerman (2025).

- identifying gaps in the current strategy and internal operations to maintain a competitive edge
- crafting a clear vision, adapting strategy, and aligning internal processes for strategic execution.

As Deming rightly points out, the system—whether aligned or misaligned—is ultimately more powerful than the individuals within it.

For an organization to perform optimally, there must be congruence—or alignment—among its strategy and its core internal components: the tasks, people, structure, and culture. Misalignment among these components can lead to performance gaps, hindering the successful implementation of strategy.

The case of VWV illustrates this powerfully: alignment between strategy and internal operations is absolutely crucial in transforming the organization. It is a key factor in determining whether your firm adapts and thrives or remains stagnant and risk failure.

This chapter will walk you through the key strategic considerations to take so that you can successfully transform your organization and achieve your ultimate vision and dreams.

Bridging Strategy and Execution: The Key to Transformation

? Where do you see your firm in 5 years from now?

Based on your vision—a compelling and ambitious picture of your firm's future state—you craft your firm's strategy and strategic goals. These could be driven by internal or external forces. For example, anticipating that firms which excel at cross-functional collaboration will thrive, you may decide to transform your firm's organizational culture, significantly changing how people collaborate and communicate with each other. Organizational transformation, then, is **internally driven**.

Often, major transformations within an organization are triggered by dynamic and rapid developments in the external environment, forcing leaders to rethink and potentially adapt their strategy. For instance, new and unexpected competitors may emerge and compete in your core market, new technologies could force you to shift the way work gets done in your firm, or regulatory changes might require altering processes. Any number of external developments may prompt a review of your strategy, guiding your actions to regain or extend your competitive advantage. In this case, a transformation within your organization is **externally driven**.

Whether triggered by external changes or initiated internally, you will drive targeted adjustments or substantial organizational transformation to **create a competitive advantage**, for example, by:

- fostering an adaptive learning culture that reaps the benefits of continuous learning for creative problem-solving and innovation

- building an agile and resilient workforce by creating an environment that supports psychological safety, encourages innovation, and enables people to embrace change
- promoting multidisciplinary collaboration to fully benefit from diverse perspectives
- developing leadership capabilities to equip leaders with the skills to navigate uncertainty, inspire teams, and drive cultural change.

Transformations within your firm can occur at different levels, ranging from firm-wide strategic shifts to more granular changes. A firm-wide strategy sets the overall direction, whether by shifting your business model, expanding into new geographic markets, transforming your organizational culture, or specializing in highly selective areas, such as large transactions. In contrast, smaller, targeted strategies focus on specific aspects of your operations to drive transformation and maintain a competitive advantage.

Whatever it is that you want to achieve, the more you **leverage a systems perspective** to align strategy with your organization's inner functioning—*"realigning your business structure, culture, and operations to adapt to internal or external changes"*[13]—the more likely you are to succeed in your effort to transform your firm.

Aligning Hard- and Software: The Congruence Model

> The degree to which the strategy, work, people, formal organization, and culture are tightly aligned will determine the organization's ability to compete and succeed.[14]

For transformation to be successful, there must be congruence—or alignment—between strategy and four core internal components: tasks, people, structure, and culture.

Without this alignment, even the best strategic plans will fail to deliver real transformation. A change in one area inevitably impacts the others.

When key components are misaligned, inefficiencies, resistance, or unintended consequences can emerge, making transformation far more difficult.

ⓘ The Congruence Model emphasizes **four key components—hardware and software—**that must be aligned to ensure that all parts of your organization are working toward common strategic goals.

Thoughtfully considering these strategic areas will help ensure that your firm's internal operations support your transformation strategy.

Developed by David Nadler, Harvard Business School Professor Michael Tushman, and Stanford Graduate School of Business Professor Charles O'Reilly,

13 Einstein (2025).
14 Mercer Delta Consulting (2004), p. 8.

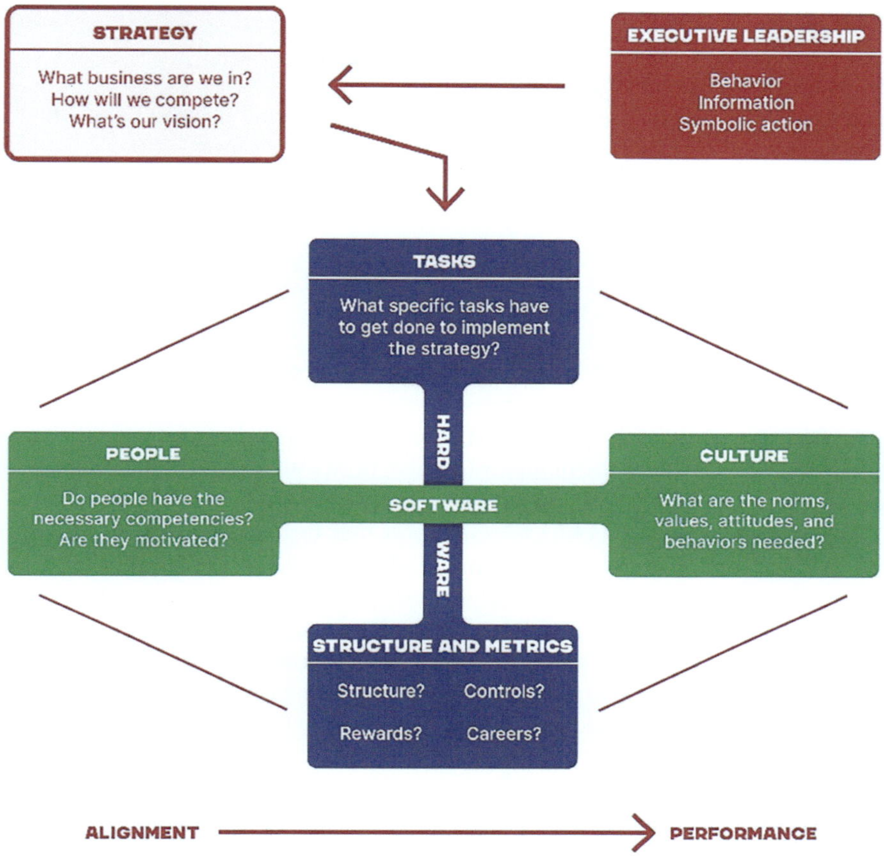

Fig. 2.1 The Congruence Model [Slightly adapted from O'Reilly III and Tushman (2021), p. 24; Einstein (2024)]

the model views organizations as dynamic systems where behavior is shaped by structures, processes, and both formal and informal organizational logics.[15]

The congruence model provides a powerful framework to:

- assess and analyze your firm's performance
- identify root causes of performance and opportunity gaps within your firm related to strategy and alignment with how your firm operates
- ensure alignment between strategy and internal operations of your firm to drive transformation success.

The components and their relationships are depicted in Fig. 2.1.

Analyzing these four areas may sound quite straightforward. However, in practice, it can be difficult to uncover blind spots unless you conduct a thorough organization analysis.

15 O'Reilly III and Tushman (2021).

Reflect and Act

Considering the congruence model:
- Which components (people, culture, tasks, structure and metrics) do you find particularly challenging in your efforts to transform your firm?
- When was the last time you spotted a misalignment among strategy, tasks, people, culture, structure and metrics that hindered transformation success?
- How did you proceed to reestablish alignment?

Leveraging the ACT Process to Align Strategy and Execution

In the first step of the ACT process (ACKNOWLEDGE), you will use the congruence model to identify performance and opportunity gaps that hinder transformation success.

In the second step (CHALLENGE), you will rethink your firm's alignment with strategy and leverage ambidextrous leadership to balance contrasting strategies, exploiting current capabilities while exploring future options simultaneously.

In the third step (TRANSFORM), you will adjust internal operations to align with the strategic goals of your transformation. As you align your transformation strategy with internal operations, it is crucial to continually monitor outcomes and adjust your approach as needed.

Acknowledge Opportunity and Performance Gaps

In a survey of 106 C-suite executives from around 17 countries, 85% agreed that their organizations were **bad at problem diagnosis**, and 87% said those mistakes carried significant costs.[16] Indeed, due to a bias for action, many leaders quickly move from analysis to solution.

The congruence model helps you conduct a **root cause analysis**, considering the entire system.

The analysis may reveal **performance gaps**, indicating that internal processes are not aligned with your strategy. Which processes will you alter? What will be the impact on other, connected factors in your firm?

Also, it may uncover **opportunity gaps**, showing that the strategy is not aligned with your external environment. The strategy may need to change, for example, because disruptive developments in the external environment have altered the competitive landscape. Having adjusted your strategy, the internal processes will need to be realigned, as a result.

Let's look at both aspects in turn.

16 Wedell-Wedellsborg (2017).

Recognize Performance Gaps in Your Internal Processes

Once you have a clear strategy, you need organizational alignment to ensure its execution. That is where identifying performance gaps comes in.

Performance gaps describe ways in which your organization underperforms, either falling short or failing to deliver on pre-defined strategic goals.

The congruence model helps you uncover misalignments between the strategy and how it is executed in practice.

Start by identifying the tasks that need to be accomplished to achieve the strategic goals. Then, determine how to align people, culture, structure and metrics to ensure execution of your strategy. Answering the following questions can help you structure the reflection:

Tasks

- What specific tasks have to be accomplished to execute our strategy?
- What interdependencies exist between tasks, and what is their impact?
- How clearly are tasks defined, and where do ambiguities exist?

People

- Do we have the right people in place to execute our strategy?
- What skills, expertise, and mindsets do we need now and in the future?
- How do we develop and retain top talent to support our long-term strategy?

Structure and metrics

- Are we measuring and rewarding the right things?
- Are there structural barriers that slow down execution or block information flow?
- Do people and teams have easy access to the critical information needed to perform?
- Do we have appropriate monitoring and control systems in place?

Culture

- Do people clearly understand the behaviors and values that drive our firm's success?
- Do people know what behaviors are expected of them to accomplish their objectives and advance their careers?
- Are cultural expectations widely shared and consistently reinforced across the firm?

Consider a law firm where the entire leadership has committed to significantly **changing the firm's leadership culture** by embracing a strong focus on developing employees. The leaders are convinced that this shift will help the firm attract and retain top talent in the future. As part of this **cultural transformation**, leadership training for all partners has been organized.

However, in the first round of trainings, 10 out of 20 nominated leaders fail to attend.

Now, assume you are the Managing Partner.

? How would you respond?

Following a **linear line of thinking**, where you seek simple cause-and-effect relationships, you might ask, *"Who didn't comply?"* and focus on identifying and addressing the *"guilty"* ones.

i The congruence model, however, takes a systems approach, allowing you to understand behavior in the broader context of the firm's structures, systems, and both formal and informal logics.

Instead of immediately identifying individuals, you would first ask, "*What factors might be discouraging partners from attending?*" You would then assess where your firm's current internal operations are misaligned with the strategy it aims to execute. Moving through the key components of the congruence model, you may **identify misalignments**, for example:

- **Structure and Metrics**

Neither your reward system nor your performance management incentivizes participation in the training. Instead, a strong emphasis on business development and billable hours discourages partners from attending.

- **Culture**

Partners hold firm, deeply-rooted beliefs about which tasks deliver true value. Your firm's insistence on client service as the highest priority undeniably explains why they refuse to step away for training, especially when a client urgently demands their attention.

The congruence model shifts the focus away from individuals, allowing you to diagnose the deeper misalignments preventing transformation to design targeted solutions.

By systematically assessing all four components, you can determine which areas to prioritize and how best to align them with your strategic goal to shift the leadership culture.

Reflect and Act

- Where do you see misalignments between your strategy and how it is executed in your firm? Consider tasks, people, culture, structure and metrics.
- Which of these areas are creating barriers to execution, and how do they impact your firm's ability to transform?
- What concrete actions have you planned to realign the areas and ensure your strategy is successfully executed to achieve transformation success?

Detect Opportunity Gaps in Your Strategy

Opportunity gaps describe ways in which the current strategies—and with it, people, culture, tasks, and structure and metrics—*"prevent you from pursuing new markets, adopting emerging technology, or generally creating value in an innovative way."*[17]

For example, significant shifts in the external environment, such as new technologies, competitors, regulations, market trends, economic shifts, can lead to a misalignment between strategy and the demands of the external environment. Thus, you may have to revise your strategy to better reflect the external dynamic shifts.

To account for these changes in your environment, you could either adapt your strategy in smaller ways or craft a strategy to significantly change and transform your firm, such as embracing entirely new business models or attempting a major cultural transformation.

To ensure that the transformation you envision becomes a reality, internal alignment across all organizational processes is essential. Achieving alignment with your new strategy will likely require simultaneous changes to all key components of the congruence model—people, culture, tasks, structure and metrics: *"These situations call for radical, or discontinuous, change, which sometimes involves the profound overhaul of most, if not all, of the organizational components."*[18]

? What makes this overhaul of internal operations so difficult in practice?

A seemingly paradoxical dynamic: the **"success syndrome"**.[19]

Once you understand its underlying logic, you can recognize it more easily and take proactive steps to ensure you achieve alignment between transformation strategy and internal processes.

When Success Leads to Failure: Trapped by "Success Syndrome"

» When new businesses and strategies require new alignments, the risk is that the old (and successful) ways of doing things can undermine the new. In the short term, there are almost always compelling reasons to stay within the status quo.[20]

Imagine you have changed your digital strategy to account for the rise of generative AI. For your new strategy to succeed, people in your firm will need to start experi-

17 Einstein (2024).

18 Mercer Delta Consulting (2004), p. 8.

19 O'Reilly, Professor at Stanford Graduate School of Business, and Tushman, Professor at Harvard Business School, identified this phenomenon, and gave it its name, see O'Reilly III and Tushman (2021), p. 26.

20 O'Reilly III and Tushman (2021), pp. 107–108.

menting more with generative AI, attend training sessions, and be both able and willing to use their acquired skills. They will also need to collaborate more across disciplines, and some people must develop a greater appreciation for the "non-legal" perspective than ever before.

You realize that internal blockers seem to be preventing your strategy from taking off as expected. Some people, including prominent partners, seem to resist the necessary changes outright, and even those who recognize the value of the new strategy seem to be stuck.

❓ What factors are driving the resistance that stands in the way of your strategy's success?

Let's go back in time for a moment.

Your original strategy served your firm well for a long time.

Generative AI was not even on the horizon, and the firm's focus was on delivering highly individualized legal advice supported by "standard" technology. To execute your strategy effectively, you ensured **strong internal alignment**: leaders fostered a culture that reinforced those behaviors that were essential for success. You measured the right things and consistently rewarded appropriate behavior.

As a result of this successful alignment, over time, **your firm grew**.

As the organization expanded, leaders realized how important it was to maintain alignment. They learned to **tighten the alignment** by refining metrics and enhancing control and coordination.

However, a tighter alignment also increases the risk of **structural inertia**.

The people who carefully built the structures, systems, processes, and performance metrics that previously drove success are often reluctant to change them, especially when confronted with uncertain opportunities that carry the risk of failure.[21]

Moreover, **cultural inertia** can develop over time.

The longer your firm remains successful, the more deeply ingrained its norms and unwritten rules become, ensuring people understand what behaviors are rewarded and what behaviors are discouraged. This strong culture makes changes in your internal systems exponentially more difficult at the very moment when internal systems need to evolve.

ℹ **Paradoxically**, while the alignment of organizational hardware (tasks, structure and metrics) and software (culture and people) is critical to the successful execution of the strategy, it can also foster structural and cultural inertia.

This inertia can make it difficult to pivot, even when external disruptions clearly threaten the future viability of your firm.

What once made your firm successful—tight internal alignment—can become an obstacle when transformation is required.

---

21 O'Reilly III and Tushman (2021), p. 30.

Thus, even in the face of disruptive technological developments, you may find it difficult to implement a new strategy and align internal processes.

? How can you realize the transformation you envision while overcoming this inertia?

First, **diagnose where alignment has become too rigid**, preventing the flexibility needed for adaptation. Which structures, processes, or cultural norms are essential for your firm's stability, and which ones are now holding it back from adapting to ensure future success?

Second, **intentionally create targeted misalignment**—loosening alignment in specific areas to create space for adaptation. For example, you might adjust performance metrics or experiment with new incentives for behaviors that haven't been rewarded before. Shifting what gets measured and recognized often proves powerful for helping people adjust behaviors and realign with the new strategy.

Ultimately, if you aim to transform your firm which is suffering from success syndrome, you do not need to abandon alignment altogether, but realign your firm's internal processes, systems, and cultural dynamics with your new, future-oriented strategy. This will ensure your firm can compete in a dynamic, competitive environment.

Reflect and Act

As you consider a significant strategic shift that you currently aim for in your firm:

- How strongly is your firm's internal alignment—culture, people, tasks, structure and metrics—still tied to a previous strategy?
- In your view, how strongly will people resist the strategic changes you attempt to implement in relation to your firm's hard- and software?
- To what extent might your firm be experiencing *"success syndrome"*, making transformation within the firm more difficult?

Challenge Assumptions on Strategy and Alignment

By now, you have uncovered performance or opportunity gaps and recognized the paradox of the success syndrome, where your firm's longstanding success makes it more difficult to transform internal processes.

To deepen your analysis, it is essential to discuss to what extent current internal operations still serve and enable—or hinder—the firm's strategic goals. This requires challenging the underlying assumptions that shape the expressed perspectives.

The following questions may support your strategic conversation:

Tasks: Are We Working on the Right Things in the Right Way?

- Are we focusing on those tasks that create the most value for our clients?
- How efficiently are we executing critical tasks? Where do bottlenecks and inefficiencies arise?
- Are we using our talent optimally, or are key individuals stuck in low-value tasks that could be delegated or automated?
- In what ways can technology enhance how we work?
- If we were designing our firm's workflows from scratch today, what would we do differently?

People: Are We Developing the Right Talent for the Future?

- How well do our current leadership and talent development efforts align with our strategic priorities?
- What skills, mindsets, or leadership qualities are missing in our firm that could accelerate transformation?
- What new leadership capabilities will we need in the future?
- How can we ensure that we are developing the next generation of leaders?
- Where do we see resistance to change? What underlying concerns or systemic barriers might be fueling it?

Structure and Metrics: Are We Still Measuring and Rewarding the Right Things?

- What behaviors and outcomes do our current compensation and reward systems reinforce?
- Are compensation and promotion systems aligned with our strategic goals?
- Are compensation and promotion systems rewarding the behaviors needed for transformation?
- How well does our decision-making structure enable agility and innovation?
- Where do we see disconnects between strategy, execution, and accountability?

Culture: Is Our Culture Enabling or Blocking the Strategy and Envisioned Transformation?

- What unwritten rules shape behaviors in our firm? Are these rules helping or hindering our transformation efforts?
- How does our culture respond to risk-taking, innovation, and experimentation?
- Do we have an environment where people feel safe to experiment, take risks, and challenge ideas, or do we shut down change before it starts?
- Do we reward continuous learning, including learning from mistakes?
- Are we unintentionally reinforcing behaviors that no longer serve our strategy?

Reflect and Act

When contemplating a major change you plan to implement in your firm:
- Which internal operations (culture, people, tasks, structure and metrics) are affected by that shift?
- What topics, questions, or concerns frequently come up when discussing necessary adaptation of internal operations?
- How do you intend to change internal operations to ensure effective execution of the strategy?

Your conversation may reveal that while you encourage experimentation, swift action, and acceptance of mistakes in some areas, risk and experimentation are deemed dangerous and must be avoided in others.

This is when **ambidextrous leadership** might be needed.

Aligning Dual Strategies with Ambidextrous Leadership

Law firm leaders often face a **dual challenge in transformation**, not just aligning one strategy with internal operations but managing two (or more) distinct strategies simultaneously. One focuses on **exploiting the current business model**, optimizing existing processes for efficiency and profitability. The other is about **exploring potential new business models**, requiring experimentation, innovation, and a tolerance for uncertainty.

Exploitation might involve leveraging existing expertise to provide high-quality legal services, maximizing billable hours, and maintaining a culture that prioritizes legal excellence and risk reduction.

Exploration might involve developing new business models, adopting generative AI, and experimenting with alternative pricing structures.

A recent white paper by Simon-Kucher & Partners, produced in collaboration with the Bucerius Center on the Legal Profession, explored how generative AI will disrupt the traditional commercial model of law firms.[22] The authors suggest that law firms must *"adopt a plurality of business and commercial models"*[23]—underscoring the urgent need for leaders to **balance exploitation and exploration to stay competitive**.

Each strategy demands a different internal alignment—tasks, structure and metrics, people, and culture must be adjusted to support short-term stability and long-term reinvention.

This tension makes strategic leadership in law firms uniquely complex and requires a deliberate approach to balancing both imperatives.

---

22 Simon-Kucher & Partners in collaboration with Bucerius Center on the Legal Profession (2025).
23 Simon-Kucher & Partners in collaboration with Bucerius Center on the Legal Profession (2025), p. 24.

Solving this dual challenge requires what is known as **ambidextrous leadership**: balancing two or more seemingly contradictory strategies.

When they are successful, it means that ambidextrous leaders have managed to build an **ambidextrous organization**—one that simultaneously exploits existing capabilities in mature markets while exploring new opportunities in emerging ones.[24]

By design, ambidextrous organizations avoid falling into the trap of success syndrome.

There are two primary approaches to crafting an ambidextrous organization.

One approach is **structural ambidexterity**, which can be seen, for example, in A&O Shearman's Innovation Hub, Fuse. In this model, a separate innovation unit explores legal tech solutions and collaborates with startups, which allows experimentation without disrupting the core business model. Since the core business and innovation units are separate, their respective internal operations can function independently, each with its own logic in terms of culture, people, tasks, structure and metrics, and this without causing confusion.

The other approach is **contextual ambidexterity**, which involves integrating innovation into daily operations without creating separate units. This approach aims to create an environment or context in which individuals are empowered to make decisions that balance both exploitation and exploration within the same organizational unit. For example, in October 2024, Clifford Chance shared insights into their early journey with generative AI and Microsoft's Copilot, reflecting their commitment to integrating advanced AI technologies into their legal practice.[25]

Exploring the intricacies of leading an ambidextrous organization would require far more space than is available here. If you are curious about how to balance exploit and explore units in your firm, I highly recommend the books "Corporate Explorer"[26] and "Lead and disrupt"[27] by the leading scholars in the field. Additionally, ▶ **Chap.** 4 of this book explores the key principle of adopting a "both/and" perspective to successfully balance the inevitable tension between exploitation and exploration—between short-term performance and long-term opportunity.

---

24 O'Reilly III and Tushman (2021), p. XV.
25 Hill (2024).
26 Binns et al. (2022).
27 O'Reilly III and Tushman (2021).

Reflect and Act

- As you lead transformation in your firm, how do you ensure your firm continues delivering high-quality legal services while creating space for innovation and new business models?
- What are your experiences with creating separate innovation units (structural ambidexterity) and embedding transformation within existing teams (contextual ambidexterity)?

Having challenged strategy and internal alignment effectively, it will be much easier for you to implement your strategy, align internal operations, and achieve the intended transformation in your firm.

Transform: Aligning Strategy and Internal Operations

By identifying performance and opportunity gaps in strategy execution, and by challenging assumptions about strategy and alignment that may hinder successful strategy implementation, you have clarified how to realign the organization to executive strategy more effectively.

Depending on your strategy, you may by now have decided to build an ambidextrous organization. The next step is to take action by adjusting internal operations and eliminating contradictions within the system.

Adjust Internal Operations to Align with Strategy and Strategic Goals of Your Transformation

To ensure alignment between strategy and internal operations, you establish **concrete activities** that help close the identified opportunity and performance gaps. Pay particular attention to eliminating any contradictions among internal operations' components.

Transformation is more likely to succeed when all four key components are aligned to support the firm's transformation strategy. You may need to make adjustments across all key components.

For example, activities might involve:

- **Tasks**

Redesign work processes to align with your strategic goals by integrating new technology or collaboration models. This might involve restructuring teams, adopting new tools, or rethinking how client work is handled.

- **People**

Develop talent through training, coaching, and succession planning, ensuring alignment with the firm's evolving needs. Invest in structured leadership selection and development to ensure your firm has the leadership needed for future growth.

- **Structure and Metrics**

Adjust decision-making and incentive systems to reinforce behaviors that support your transformation strategy.

- **Culture**

Reinforce new behaviors through leadership role modeling, storytelling, and reward systems that reinforce behaviors that align with your strategy (see also ► **Chap.** 3 to learn more about how to foster a strong and adaptive culture in your firm).

Consistently Monitor Results and Readjust Both Strategy and Internal Processes

As you align your transformation strategy with internal operations, it is crucial to continually monitor outcomes and adjust your approach as needed.

Conducting regular **evaluations** of both strategic goals and internal processes will help you remain agile in the face of emerging challenges and opportunities.

A data-driven feedback loop enables you to identify areas of strength as well as those aspects that require recalibration.

This process also cultivates a culture of continuous improvement.

By embracing an **iterative approach**, you ensure that your strategy stays in sync with both external demands and your firm's internal capabilities.

Ultimately, consistent monitoring and readjustment pave the way for sustained transformation and competitive advantage.

Summary

You have now aligned your transformation strategy with your firm's internal operations using the congruence model. This systems perspective has helped you assess and uncover blind spots in the current alignment between transformation strategy and internal operations. It has helped you realign internal operations to allow for effective strategy implementation.

This is what you have accomplished by working through the steps outlined in this chapter:

ACKNOWLEDGE To identify performance and opportunity gaps, you

- used the congruence model and assessed the level of alignment between strategy, hardware, and software.

- uncovered the dynamics behind the "success syndrome", which can lead to strategic and cultural inertia precisely when your firm needs new strategies and substantial transformation, and identified options to circumvent this inertia.

CHALLENGE To question assumptions about strategy and alignment, you
- scrutinized your firm's operations related to tasks, people, culture, structure and metrics and their impact on your strategy.
- investigated the need to balance multiple strategies, allowing you to exploit your current business while simultaneously exploring new opportunities with courage. You recognized ambidextrous leadership as essential for balancing exploitation and exploration.

TRANSFORM To align transformation strategy and internal operations, you
- adjusted internal operations, eliminating contradictions within the system, such as misalignments in compensation or incentives.
- regularly evaluated your strategic goals and internal operations, ensuring that your firm remained adaptable and responsive throughout the transformation process.

References

Ackerman, N. (2025, January 1). The secret to making AI work is to get people trained and enthused. *The Times.* https://www.thetimes.com/article/bfe6c486-5fbc-40bf-85ab-e4854982fc4a

Baksi, C. (2025, January 23). Christina Blacklaws: 'I'd love to see firms embrace tech faster'. Interview. *The Times.* https://www.thetimes.com/uk/law/article/christina-blacklaws-id-love-to-see-firms-embrace-tech-faster-nlvw2lcrm?t=1738746053281

Binns, A., O'Reilly, C. A., III, & Tushman, M. (2022). *Corporate explorer. How corporations beat startups at the innovation game*. Wiley.

Deming, W. E. (1993). https://deming.org/a-bad-system-will-beat-a-good-person-every-time/

Einstein, B. (2024, December 17). Understanding the Congruence Model: Aligning strategy, structure, & people. *Harvard Business School online*. https://online.hbs.edu/blog/post/congruence-model

Einstein, B. (2025, January 21). Leading successful organizational transformation through culture. *Harvard Business School Online*. https://online.hbs.edu/blog/post/organizational-transformation

Hilborne, N. (2024, October 31). Law firm uses trainees to find problems and solve them with AI. *Legalfutures*. https://www.legalfutures.co.uk/latest-news/law-firm-uses-trainees-to-find-problems-and-solve-them-with-ai

Hill, C. (2024, October 22). *Clifford Chance's early generative AI and Copilot journey – The inside view. Legal IT Insider*. https://legaltechnology.com/2024/10/22/clifford-chances-early-generative-ai-and-copilot-journey-the-inside-view/?utm

McCann, K. (2024, November 29). *Embracing digital: How VWV is reshaping legal services technology magazine*. https://technologymagazine.com/company-reports/embracing-digital-how-vwv-is-reshaping-legal-services

Mercer Delta Consulting. (2004). *The Congruence Model – A roadmap for understanding organizational performance*

O'Reilly, C. A., III, & Tushman, M. L. (2021). *Lead and disrupt. How to solve the innovator's dilemma* (2nd ed.). Stanford University Press.

Robin AI. (n.d.). Newsroom. *Young lawyers are becoming more valuable thanks to AI*. https://www.robinai.com/newsroom/young-lawyers-are-becoming-more-valuable-thanks-to-ai

Simon-Kucher & Partners in collaboration with Bucerius Center on the Legal Profession. (2025). The AI-Conomics of legal services. How generative AI will transform the commercial model of law

Wedell-Wedellsborg, T. (2017). Are you solving the right problems? Reframing them can reveal unexpected solutions. *Harvard Business Review, 95*(*1-2*), 76–83.

Williams, R. (2023, July 3). How law firms are approaching AI and its impact within the Commercial Property Sector. *VWV*. https://www.vwv.co.uk/news-and-events/blog/property-law-brief/ai-commercial-property?utm

Shaping an Adaptive Culture to Build a Future-Ready Firm

Contents

M. Bernhardt, *Leading Transformation in Law Firms*, Law for Professionals,
https://doi.org/10.1007/978-3-031-98653-6_3

» Culture always wins.[1]

When Satya Nadella stepped in as Microsoft's CEO in 2014, he inherited a culture so combative and siloed that it threatened the very future of the company. Its command-and-control culture had promoted risk aversion and internal politics and had severely hampered cross-divisional collaboration.

Nadella intuitively understood that his company's future success was inextricably linked to its ability to transform its culture—a point underscored by McGuire and Palus in their quote about the critical importance of culture. Nadella recognized that the company needed a **culture transformation**—in that case **a shift toward a growth mindset** where everyone embraced continuous learning, risk-taking, and the opportunity to learn from failure.[2]

This cultural transformation had to begin at the top, with leaders fully supporting and embodying the new culture.

ℹ One of the most successful ways to drive significant change in your firm is through cultural transformation.

Leveraging your firm's culture to achieve strategic goals has always been crucial, but it becomes even more critical in today's dynamic environment. As a leader, you are likely to drive transformation initiatives more frequently, and across various areas of your firm, demanding that individuals and teams are prepared and able to swiftly adapt to changing internal requirements.

A strong and adaptive culture is what enables individuals and teams to meet these demands, making your firm more capable of achieving the envisioned changes.

Often, transforming your firm's culture is essential to ensure the success of other transformation initiatives. For example:

- adopting new commercial models: systematically integrating value-based pricing alongside a billable-hour model requires lawyers, who are often accustomed to competing on billable hours, to embrace collaboration and shared accountability.
- implementing AI-driven tools across the firm: introducing advanced technologies can threaten long-standing traditions, thus creating resistance. A culture that values lifelong learning—including from mistakes—and open-mindedness is vital to help people embrace and fully leverage new technologies.
- adopting hybrid or virtual work: moving to flexible work arrangements can raise concerns about accountability and ownership. Leaders must strengthen trust within their teams and foster honest, open communication to adapt successfully.

Perhaps the most pressing cultural transformation in the near future—especially for firms with very limited steering and management structures—may arise from the need to gradually shift toward being led and managed more like a corporation. A

1 McGuire and Palus (2018), p. 146.
2 Ibarra and Scoular (2019).

recent white paper by Simon-Kucher & Partners, in collaboration with the Bucerius Center on the Legal Profession, explores how generative AI will disrupt law firms' traditional business models.[3]

It argues that, moving forward, law firms may need to operate more like corporations, adopting a greater division of labor, more centralized management, and a broader range of commercial models.[4]

This implies that partners need to be willing to give up control and decision-making power and foster collaboration with both legal and *"non-legal"* professionals.

Based on interviews with Managing Partners, the white paper's authors emphasize how substantial this shift in organizational culture is expected to be:

> **This cultural change is seen as the number one challenge by Managing Partners**, ranking well ahead of technical obstacles or imperfections in the technology itself.[5]

Regardless of the specific transformation you pursue in your firm, ensuring your firm's culture aligns with your transformation goals—clearly and consistently supporting them—will likely be a cornerstone of success.

Let us explore how to shape an adaptive culture that nurtures continuous learning and sustainably unlocks peak performance.

Organizational Culture Is the Soil for Any Transformation

> Most leaders focus on structure, systems, processes, metrics, and rewards. But culture often spells the difference between success and failure.[6]

Despite its strong impact on organizational performance and competitive advantage, senior leaders often find it difficult to shape a culture that enables adaptation in today's rapidly changing world:

- **94%** of more than 7000 executives surveyed by Deloitte believe that a distinct workplace culture is essential for business success.[7]
- Only **12%** of executives feel their companies drive the "right culture."[8]
- A study by the Institute of Corporate Productivity found that just **15%** of companies surveyed succeeded in transforming their culture.[9]

Often, organizational culture is perceived as an inherently complex and abstract concept, making it difficult to influence it in meaningful ways.

3 Simon-Kucher & Partners in collaboration with Bucerius Center on the Legal Profession (2025).
4 Simon-Kucher & Partners in collaboration with Bucerius Center on the Legal Profession (2025).
5 Simon-Kucher & Partners in collaboration with Bucerius Center on the Legal Profession (2025), p. 14 [emphasis added].
6 Einstein (2025).
7 Deloitte USA (2012).
8 Deloitte USA (2012).
9 Goodrich (2019).

? So, what is culture?

Culture is *"a set of norms and values that are widely shared and strongly held throughout the organization"*.[10] When values are translated into norms and into day-to-day actions, culture is reflected in *"the pattern of behavior that people and systems reinforce over time."*[11]

Organizations establish specific **values** that form the foundation for **cultural norms**—the standards for behavior. These norms help interpret and evaluate events, clarifying appropriate and inappropriate behaviors. **Culture becomes visible through the behaviors** that the firm rewards, whether formally or informally.

Culture influences virtually every aspect of your firm:

How people think and make decisions, how they interact and work together, how they communicate, what they value, and how the organization performs daily. And leaders' behaviors play the most critical role in shaping and cultivating that culture.[12]

Transformations Require a Strong and Adaptive Culture

» Success in the Age of AI will largely depend on an organization's ability to learn and change faster than it ever has before.[13]

For organizations facing rapid and radical change, staying competitive depends on constantly learning. This organizational ability is the hallmark of a **learning organization,**[14] one that is *"skilled at creating, acquiring, and transferring knowledge, and at modifying its behavior to reflect new knowledge and insights."*[15]

A learning organization systematically fosters the learning of its members across the firm, drives innovation,[16] and continuously transforms itself to adapt to new challenges. *Systems thinking* is a cornerstone of the learning organization (see ▶ **Chap.** 2 for how to apply systems thinking in relation to strategic alignment).

To build a learning organization, it is essential to cultivate a **learning culture**[17] that embeds learning at the individual, team, and organizational levels, encouraging people to try new things and learn from failure.

Organizations with a strong learning culture demonstrate:

- greater transformation capacity, enabling quick responses to changing business conditions[18]

10 O'Reilly and Chatman (1996).
11 O'Reilly (2024), p. 42.
12 O'Reilly (2024), p. 42.
13 Candelon et al. (2023).
14 Senge (1990).
15 Garvin (1993).
16 Achdiat et al. (2023).
17 Schein (1992).
18 Daly and Ahmetaj (2020).

- improved performance at both individual and organizational levels[19]
- higher motivation, satisfaction, engagement, and commitment among members[20]
- increased retention
- greater innovation and creativity[21]
- effective problem-solving
- enhanced efficiency, profitability, and growth.[22]

Learning and adaptability are interdependent, each facilitating the other.

Adaptability refers to an organization's capacity to effectively respond to external changes and adjust practices to meet challenges and opportunities. It is considered *"**the critical success factor during periods of transformation** and systemic change. It allows us to be **faster and better at learning**, and it orients us toward the opportunities ahead, not just the challenges."*[23]

Organizations that foster adaptability outperform those that neglect it.[24]

In dynamic environments characterized by rapid technological changes, **a strong learning culture improves company performance**—provided members comprehensively embrace adaptability as a norm.[25]

Critical elements of adaptability include:

- curiosity
- continuous learning
- high risk tolerance
- willingness to experiment
- initiative
- agility.

Building a strong culture—where organizational members consistently uphold shared norms—that emphasizes adaptability is essential to drive change and transformation.

Leadership Shapes and Transforms the Organizational Culture

> Organizations don't outperform their leaders… they reflect them.[26]

19 Daly and Ahmetaj (2020).
20 Joo and Shim (2010) and Halmaghi and Todăriță (2023).
21 Achdiat et al. (2023) and Halmaghi and Todăriță (2023).
22 Daly and Ahmetaj (2020) and Halmaghi and Todăriță (2023).
23 Brassey et al. (2021) [emphasis added].
24 Chatman et al. (2014).
25 Chatman et al. (2014).
26 Clark (2020) (Kindle version), p. 39 [location 468].

Leadership is crucial in shaping and cultivating a positive organizational culture. Leaders' values, attitudes, and behaviors set the tone for everyone within the organization.

To effectively shape the organizational culture, leadership must

- role-model desired behaviors consistently.[27]
- measure and reward behaviors that align with the desired culture.
- allocate resources to reinforce the desired culture.
- uncover and shift deep-rooted assumptions to align with the future culture.
- continuously offer support and resources to help individuals and teams adapt to changes.
- clearly communicate the expected behaviors and mindsets.[28]

When you realize that your culture needs to evolve to make your firm future-ready, it is helpful to think of this process as a long-distance effort. Any cultural shift needs to be consistently reinforced so that people see it and believe that you mean it. Like any long-distance journey, it begins with recognizing the challenge, preparing thoroughly, and taking the first step.

The ACT Process: Culture Is the Cornerstone of Any Transformation

In the first step of the process (ACKNOWLEDGE), you begin by evaluating your firm's current culture and identifying gaps in its capacity to adapt and thrive during transformation. You pay particular attention to how people think about and whether they (avoid to) discuss failure and learning within the organization. People's perceptions likely influence their level of learning and adaptability.

In the second step (CHALLENGE), you question the underlying assumptions about failure and performance, as well as the emotions that may obstruct the development of a more adaptive culture. You foster a safe environment where team members feel encouraged to discuss mistakes openly (see also ▶ **Chap.** 5 on fostering psychological safety). This openness enhances group learning and strengthens collective problem-solving capabilities.

In the third step (TRANSFORM), you implement the "LEASH" model—developed by Stanford Graduate School of Business Professor Charles O'Reilly—to drive culture transformation systemically. The model provides guidance on how leadership behaviors, employee involvement, rewards, stories, and HR systems can be aligned with the desired culture. Finally, investing in consistent leadership development will ensure that cultural change remains sustainable.

27 Schein and Schein (2017).
28 Jerab and Mabrouk (2023).

Reflect and Act

- What cultural imperatives exist in your organization? Which behaviors does your firm reward, and which does it sanction?
- How strongly does your culture emphasize adaptability as a success factor for confronting change?
- In what ways might your firm's culture need to change to become more adaptive?

Acknowledge Gaps in Learning and Adaptability

? How adaptive and flexible is your firm currently?

? To what extent does your culture reward learning, seizing opportunities, and taking smart risks?

First, it's essential to understand your culture's nuances, particularly how assumptions about failure and learning impact adaptability.

Assess Your Firm's Culture

Diagnostic instruments can provide valuable insights into your firm's cultural system by offering a holistic view. For example, the "Organizational Culture Audit" (OCA™), developed by the Kets De Vries Institute,[29] a renowned provider and recognized industry leader in supporting global leaders in high-performance organizations, analyzes 12 key dimensions of culture, including trust, teamwork, change orientation, and the learning environment. This audit reveals discrepancies between the organization's stated values and actual behaviors, uncovering hidden cultural dynamics that may impede current or future transformation efforts.

Employee surveys are another effective way to identify cultural strengths and areas needing improvement.

To shape a culture that emphasizes learning and adaptability, it is essential that leaders consistently model these behaviors—in both words and actions. For example, their assumptions about failure and risk-taking can foster or stymie the development of adaptive behaviors.

However, leaders often find it difficult to shape a culture where learning from failure includes openly discussing and sharing mistakes. They feel there is a danger inherent in promoting tolerance for mistakes and ask:

29 Kets de Vries Institute (n.d.).

- How can I address failures constructively while maintaining high-performance standards?
- How do I avoid creating a laissez-faire culture where recurring basic mistakes become acceptable?

Answering these crucial questions—both for yourself and among your firm's entire leadership—is a prerequisite for shaping a learning culture.

Why We Fail to Learn from Failure

To err is human—and we don't like it.

According to Harvard Business School professor Amy C. Edmondson,[30] there are **three main reasons** why organizations don't fully leverage mistakes as learning opportunities:

1. **Aversion** to failure
2. **Confusion** about failure types
3. **Fear** of rejection for having failed.

Let us look at each one in turn.

1. Aversion to Failure

Failure can threaten our sense of ego and perceived competence. The fear of appearing incompetent often triggers defensive behaviors such as blame-shifting.

Admitting mistakes can be especially challenging in the legal profession, where quality is often synonymous with perfection and absolute flawlessness. Falling short of these high standards can evoke feelings of shame and embarrassment. Because these feelings are deeply uncomfortable, we often avoid sharing our failures.

Reflect and Act

- What are your automatic thoughts and emotions when reflecting on your past failures?
- What factors make it easier or more challenging for you to share your mistakes openly?
- In what situations do you show empathy toward those who admit mistakes, and when do you find yourself reacting more critically?
- What is one specific behavior you could demonstrate to make it easier for individuals or teams to admit mistakes?

30 Edmondson (2023) (Kindle version), p. 25 [373].

3

■ 2. Confusion About Failure Types

An important reason why it is so difficult to create a culture that fully leverages learning from mistakes—thereby enhancing adaptability and performance—is the lack of clarity surrounding different types of failures.

According to Amy Edmondson, it is essential to distinguish between **three types of failures** and **contexts**:

- basic failure
- complex failure
- intelligent failure
- consistent, predictable context
- variable context
- novel context.[31]

Basic failures often occur in **consistent, predictable contexts** where sufficient knowledge and information are available. For example, failing to proofread a document, forgetting to return a client's call, or texting while driving are basic failures in predictable contexts.

Complex failures tend to happen in **variable contexts** with multiple interacting factors. For instance, a train might be heavily delayed due to a sudden storm or a health incident onboard. Imagine you planned for contingencies but still missed an important meeting due to cascading disruptions: this qualifies as a complex failure in a variable context.

Intelligent failures are likely to occur in **novel contexts** where experimentation is necessary to find solutions. For example, more than 90% of newly developed drugs fail in clinical trials. You cannot prevent intelligent failures, nor should you try. They propel innovation and provide answers—or better questions—for tackling challenges. By cognitively and emotionally accepting them, you can better leverage this type of failure for growth.

Regardless of the type of failure and context, it is important to acknowledge the mistake and consider what actions can be taken to prevent similar occurrences.

However, not all failures merit celebration. You don't need to celebrate a basic mistake that happened in a consistent context, and, of course, intelligent failures can also occur in consistent and variable contexts.

The phrase "fail fast and often" emphasizes the importance of **intelligent failures in novel contexts** to drive progress. Practices like "failure of the week" sessions and "f*-up nights", where professionals openly share stories of their failures and what they learned from them, focus on sharing intelligent failures in novel contexts that boost learning, development, innovation, and personal and organizational growth.

■ 3. Fear of Rejection for Having Failed

We are social creatures who depend on being part of a group or a team, and most of us seek appreciation from those around us.

---

31 Edmondson (2023) (Kindle version), p. 223 [location 3299].

When we make mistakes, the level of **psychological safety** within a team significantly influences whether we feel comfortable admitting them (see also ▶ **Chap.** 5 on how to foster psychological safety in teams). As Edmondson states: *"Psychological safety helps us do and say the things that allow us to learn and make progress in our changing, uncertain world."*[32]

In teams with **low psychological safety,** we tend to ignore, dismiss, or deny our failures. We would rather blame others than admit our mistakes because we fear being "punished" for them. This "punishment" can range from minor social consequences—such as disapproving looks or being asked, *"Why on earth did you do that?"*—to more significant ones, like being excluded from future projects or losing a previously held role.

Conversely, in teams with **high levels of psychological safety**, people feel comfortable asking questions, making suggestions, voicing concerns, and admitting mistakes without fear of judgment. This environment also encourages team members to ask for help, which can prevent or mitigate failures before they escalate. Psychological safety reduces anxiety and defensiveness,[33] creating a supportive environment for behavior changes necessary to meet shifting organizational demands. Teams with higher psychological safety experience lower levels of emotional exhaustion, a key predictor of job performance.[34] Moreover, psychological safety allows team members to report errors quickly, thus avoiding more severe consequences.

Reflect and Act

Thinking about a transformation you currently aim for:

- How do you typically respond to failure—your own and others?
- What kind of failures—yours and others'—have cost you the most time so far?
- In what contexts did they occur?
- Unless they were intelligent failures in novel contexts, what steps can you—and others—take to prevent similar mistakes in the future?

Challenge Assumptions About Failure and High Performance

» If you want best practices, you need best beliefs. Beliefs drive practices.[35]

Once you have identified potential misalignments between your current culture and what is needed to achieve sustainable success, it is essential to examine and challenge specific assumptions that might impede a cultural shift. Deeply ingrained beliefs about failure and performance can hinder the creation of a highly adaptive culture. Also, a crucial step in strengthening an adaptive culture is to foster an environment where open communication about mistakes encourages group learning.

32 Edmondson (2023) (Kindle version), p. 38 [location 592].
33 Zhou and Chen (2021).
34 Zhou and Chen (2021).
35 McGuire and Palus (2018), p. 145.

Counter the Aversion to Making Mistakes

First, help others reframe their perception of failure.

We experience reality through cognitive frames: clusters of assumptions that shape our thinking.[36] Sometimes, it is helpful to challenge these frames and adopt new ones. Framing failure as *"bad"* immediately triggers defensive reactions. By pausing and focusing on what we can learn from the experience, we reframe the failure more productively. Instead of asking, *"Why did I do it?"*, we can ask, *"What can I learn from this to avoid repeating it?"* or *"What can we, as a team, learn from this?"* Asking better questions can help us embrace the fact that we all make mistakes, without downplaying them.

Second, help others transition from striving for perfection to aiming for excellence.

Perfectionism can prevent us from accepting failure, and, as a result, from reaching our full potential—a particularly risky limitation in a fast-changing world. Focusing on excellence allows us to set realistic goals and appreciate progress rather than fixating solely on results. Interestingly, we tend to respect people who admit their errors more than those who claim never to make mistakes. Ironically, perfection often makes us less likable.

Third, foster a "growth mindset" to shift perspectives on failure and learning.

This shift typically takes some time, and leadership must make developing a growth mindset a strategic priority to embed it at every level of the organization (see also ▶ **Chap.** 8 on how to adopt a growth mindset).

During the interviews for this book, one interviewee shared their experience leading such a process, **convincing the partnership that embedding a growth mindset across the firm would enable the firm's future growth**—the firm's primary strategic goal—and prepare them for an ever-evolving future.

Counter the Confusion Around Failure Types

Together with your team, **discuss failure types and context**. Explore what team members consider basic, complex, and intelligent failures, as well as predictable, variable, or novel contexts.

This differentiation helps your team understand that failure, while not always desirable, can be valuable and isn't inherently dangerous or detrimental.

Also, help your team deepen their skill to assess which type of failure is acceptable in a particular situation[37] by considering the following two questions:

? How certain or uncertain is the situation?

36 Edmondson (2023) (Kindle version), p. 183 [location 2710].
37 Edmondson (2023) (Kindle version), p. 202 [location 2986].

Consider how much you know about the situation and how familiar the context is. If the context is predictable and the situation is well-understood, you can rely on established approaches. If the context is novel and the situation is uncertain, experimentation becomes necessary, as you cannot draw on existing knowledge.

? What is at stake?

Assess the level of risk: is it negligible, moderate, or high? When the stakes are high, you will take smaller risks. As the context becomes more uncertain and novel, the likelihood of mistakes increases.

Develop strategies for addressing various types of failures. How can you:

- prevent basic failures as much as possible (e.g., by focusing on preparation and attention to detail)
- anticipate complex failures (e.g., by identifying potential risks and planning how to mitigate them)
- embrace intelligent failures with curiosity and openness?

Foster continuous team reflection to advance learning from mistakes.

Counter the Fear of Rejection

First, discuss failure openly while ensuring accountability.

This helps reduce the fear of admitting failure due to the perceived risk of being "punished". As previously mentioned, leaders may find it challenging to foster psychological safety and shape a culture where learning from failure includes openly discussing and sharing mistakes—due to a perceived discrepancy between tolerating failure and ensuring high-performance standards.

Edmondson emphasizes that high levels of psychological safety and high performance standards go hand in hand, stating:

> I'd go so far as to say that **insisting on high standards without psychological safety is a recipe for failure**—and not the good kind. People are more likely to mess up (even for things they know how to do well) when they're stressed.[38]

Intelligent failures can only lead to learning when people feel safe sharing them. Otherwise, these failures lose their potential to drive improvement, and people may repeat them. This is why fostering a psychologically safe environment is a crucial prerequisite for allowing people to openly admit their mistakes.

Second, remind yourself that fostering psychological safety and a growth mindset go hand in hand.

Psychological safety is closely linked to a growth mindset. With a fixed mindset, you won't promote psychological safety because sharing mistakes threatens your self-esteem.

38 Edmondson (2023) (Kindle version), p. 40 [location 611] [emphasis added].

Transform: Key Levers to Fully Un-LEASH Culture Shift

O'Reilly found that leaders in strong-culture organizations use **five common levers** to shape and shift organizational culture, which he subsequently called the **LEASH model**.[39] These levers are based on the psychological dynamics of strong cultures with well-defined expectations for appropriate behavior. All levers benefit from a strong **positive emotional climate** in your firm. Thus, recognizing the significant potential of positive emotions and fostering a positive emotional culture will lay the foundation for the five levers in the LEASH model to fully unleash their power.

Positive Emotions Are Contagious: Build Your Firm's Emotional Culture

Emotions in the workplace aren't just individual experiences; they are contagious. They spread across the organization as people subconsciously pick up nonverbal cues from others, leading their emotional states to converge.[40] This is how they shape your organization's emotional culture.

Barsade and O'Neill[41] describe a **positive emotional culture** as one where employees feel safe expressing emotions, taking risks, and learning without fear of rejection or blame.

To shape this kind of positive culture, it is essential that you **model and reinforce positive emotions** through your actions and communication.

Typically, when we think of failure, it triggers negative emotions like discomfort, insecurity, or guilt.

? How different might failure feel if it sparked excitement, joy, or curiosity instead?

Benjamin Zander, the Boston Philharmonic Orchestra conductor, always encouraged his students to celebrate mistakes by throwing their arms in the air and shouting, *"Fantastic, I made a mistake!"* This apparently playful (and a bit silly) exercise shifted the original emotions and promoted a positive response to failure. Students embraced mistakes as opportunities to grow, creating an atmosphere of contagious positive energy and focused learning.

Make no mistake: fostering positive emotions is not just a feel-good strategy. **Fostering positive emotions is fundamental to building a highly adaptive learning culture**.

Emotions shape every aspect of workplace behavior.

Positive emotions, such as excitement, curiosity, joy, contentment, empathy, hope, and gratitude, are key to strengthening:

- a willingness to embrace, discuss, and learn from failure

39 O'Reilly (2024), p. 42.
40 Hatfield et al. (1994).
41 Barsade and O'Neill (2016).

- high psychological safety within teams
- an individual and a collective growth mindset across the entire firm.

Research links positive emotions to:
- increased willingness to tackle challenges[42]
- increased willingness to pursue entrepreneurial opportunities[43]
- greater persistence when facing setbacks[44]—helping teams stay focused even in tough times
- a positive impact on cognition: positive emotions broaden attention[45] and thought patterns,[46] they help us recognize opportunities more quickly, and boost creativity
- enhanced motivation and productivity[47]—for example, an experimental study found that productivity levels rose by 12% when employees experienced positive affect[48]
- stronger favorable reactions to others that strengthen social connection[49]
- an undoing effect on negative emotions,[50] which is essential for navigating emotional challenges that often occur during transformation.

Moreover, a high ratio of positive to negative emotions is associated with an organization's **higher profitability**.[51] Studies suggest that an optimal balance occurs when individuals experience approximately three to five times more positive than negative emotions. One reason for this ratio is that we all experience negative emotions more strongly than positive ones. Therefore, to counter these negative effects, you have to ensure that you display and support positive emotions and provide concrete, positive feedback often.

Reflect and Act

Take a moment to reflect on your recent interactions:
- How many involved positive emotions like excitement, joy, or empathy?
- How many were dominated by negative emotions like frustration or stress?
- What strategies can you use to cultivate positive emotions in your firm, especially during those times when transformation becomes particularly challenging?

---

42 Diener et al. (2002).
43 Chen et al. (2021).
44 Haidt (2000).
45 Fredrickson and Branigan (2005).
46 Isen (1987).
47 Martin (2004).
48 Oswald et al. (2015).
49 Haidt (2000).
50 Sekerka and Fredrickson (2008).
51 Sekerka and Fredrickson (2008).

Un-LEASH Culture Transformation

A crucial driver of Satya Nadella's success in transforming Microsoft's culture was his relentless focus on developing a growth mindset. To achieve this substantial shift, Nadella utilized **five mechanisms, encapsulated in the acronym LEASH**, based on a model developed by Stanford Business School Professor Charles A. O'Reilly.[52]

L: Leader Actions

As we have seen, leadership behaviors are the most critical factor in shaping organizational culture. Your actions—what you say, do, prioritize, and ignore—send strong signals about what is valued. People closely observe your behavior to determine how they should act to be successful. Over time, they will adjust their behavior to align with your example.

If you aim to create an environment of psychological safety—where the growth mindset is lived and where positive emotions are prioritized—you must intentionally act, speak, and think accordingly.

As Jack Welch, former CEO of General Electric, famously said, leaders have to be **relentless in sending the same message and boring in repeating it**. By consistently sending the same signals, you enable people to learn quickly and effectively what is expected of them. The clearer and more consistent your signals, the stronger the culture will be.

? How do you get the entire leadership on board?

The structure of law firm leadership demands a collective approach to cultural transformation. Success depends on engaging the entire partnership and leadership team. Every leader should:

- recognize the costs of the current culture.
- know which behaviors promote transformation.
- have access to a strong support system to adapt leadership behaviors and foster a growth mindset.

Satya Nadella initiated several key measures, including the following:

- Nadella required his senior leadership team to read the book "Nonviolent Communication", setting a clear tone that yelling and disrespectful communication had no place in the company.
- He spent the first 9 months in his new role conducting a "listening tour" using various formats, such as focus groups, pulse checks, and surveys, to understand employees' perspectives.
- As a clear signal regarding priorities, the company tagline shifted from *"a computer on every desk"* to *"empower every person and organization."*[53]

52 O'Reilly (2024), p. 42.
53 O'Reilly (2024), p. 45.

- He redesigned the performance management system, shifting it from a model that encouraged internal competition to one that rewarded learning and cooperation.
- He invested in leadership training to ensure leaders modeled the desired culture, focusing on developing employees.

▪ E: Employee Involvement

Culture transformation requires genuine employee involvement. When employees feel sincerely included, they are more likely to view the transformation as "theirs" rather than an initiative imposed from above. Authentic involvement—in contrast to fake involvement—creates **psychological ownership,**[54] which drives the motivation to improve and nurture the envisioned culture.

Psychological ownership consists of four elements:

- self-efficacy: people's beliefs in their ability to succeed in tasks and take practical actions[55]
- accountability: the expectation of being held accountable and the right to hold others accountable[56]
- belongingness: feeling connected to the organization, "having a place", meeting both social and emotional needs[57]
- self-identity: feeling that the envisioned culture affirms one's values and identity.[58]

Moreover, **organizational identity** plays a crucial role. It involves the shared beliefs about what the firm stands for and what it should stand for: it is your firm's DNA. In essence, it answers questions such as:

- Who are we as a firm? Who do we want to become?
- What are our core values?
- How do we create value?
- What does success look like for us as a firm?
- How do others experience us as an organization?

Whether you aim to transform your firm's culture, or pursue a transformation unrelated to it, whenever people feel that the very essence of what the firm stands for—its **organizational DNA**—is at risk, they are likely to resist the envisioned changes.

For example, the white paper by Simon-Kucher & Partners in collaboration with the Bucerius Center on the Legal Profession posited that *"the fundamental requirement for greater deployment of Gen AI tools and efficiency gains will be*

54 Avey et al. (2009).
55 Bandura (1997).
56 Lerner and Tetlock (1999).
57 Avey et al. (2009).
58 Bandura (1997).

productization."[59] It further stated that *"legal professionals often view productization as antithetical to their profession"*.

This observation is consistently reflected in research:

> » A strategic change such as altering the value proposition of an organization may have profound implications for how individuals, groups, and organizations think of who they are and what they do.[60]

3

Therefore, when you begin discussing productization and encounter strong, negative emotions, it is worth considering how issues of identity may be involved. Only then can you address people's real concerns. Otherwise, you risk engaging in a pseudo-discussion that entirely misses the point.

Nadella actively increased employee involvement, e.g., through frequent pulse checks, monthly town hall meetings, and focus groups with employees from different generations and diverse backgrounds to discuss which cultural elements to preserve and which ones to leave behind. The annual meeting format was transformed from a series of speeches and presentations into a 5-day hackathon with active employee participation and idea-sharing.

▪ A: Aligned Rewards

The behavior that gets measured and rewarded is the behavior that gets repeated.

? Is your reward system aligned with the behaviors expected in the future culture?

This question needs to be answered honestly.

While monetary rewards are important, they often *"come too infrequently to reinforce specific behaviors."*[61] More effective rewards include, for example:

- Recognition: verbal praise, promotion, symbolic rewards (e.g., certificates), delivered with sincerity.
- Celebration of "intelligent failures", e.g., through playful rituals.

The most dangerous pitfall is failing to align formal monetary rewards with what you claim you reward or with the existing informal rewards. If teamwork is declared essential but non-collaborative individuals are promoted, employees will quickly learn that collaboration is not what truly matters.

INSEAD professor Herminia Ibarra highlights how Allen & Overy (now A&O Shearman) **abandoned year-end appraisals and rankings that conflicted with their vision for a learning culture**. They realized that the appraisals contradicted the desired open and supportive conversations. What did they do instead? They sup-

---

59 Simon-Kucher & Partners in collaboration with Bucerius Center on the Legal Profession (2025), p. 15.

60 Whitley et al. (2014), p. 18.

61 O'Reilly (2024), p. 44.

ported partners *"to engage year-round in coaching conversations with associates, providing them real-time feedback on their work."*[62]

- **S: Stories, Signals, and Vivid Illustrations**

Stories convey powerful cognitive and emotional messages, illustrating the behaviors and mindsets necessary for the intended culture. Stories told by leaders and employees serve as vivid examples of what is valued, expected, and rewarded.

At Microsoft, leaders were instructed to begin each meeting by sharing a story about an employee or customer whose accomplishments illustrated the company's growth mindset values, thus reinforcing the importance of a growth-oriented culture.[63]

Signals also illustrate a culture's embedded values:

- Office design: How are different spaces furnished?
- Dress Codes: What clothing do people wear? Does the culture encourage diversity or conformity in professional attire?
- Space allocation: Who gets the large, bright corner office?

- **H: HR System Alignment**

It is essential to have HR systems that are deliberately aligned with the goals of cultural transformation. Recruitment, selection, training, rewards, and promotions should all reinforce the behaviors the desired culture seeks to cultivate.

For example, ensure that you:

- recruit for culture fit: avoid hiring individuals who don't align with your cultural values, even if they bring immediate business benefits.
- don't compromise: for example, a lateral hire with a strong book of business but poor leadership skills can significantly harm your culture, and, over time, the financial bottom line.
- enforce cultural standards: do not retain individuals—whether employees or leaders— who consistently fail to align with the firm's culture and values.

Additionally, focus on **developing future leaders** early on and consistently to allow them to model appropriate behaviors. Prioritize cultural alignment in every selection and promotion process.

Summary

With the help of diagnostic tools, you have gained clarity about your firm's cultural gaps. You have deepened your understanding of mindset traps related to failure and learning.

62 Ibarra and Scoular (2019), p. 117.
63 O'Reilly (2024).

You have challenged and adapted the assumptions about failure and performance that can hinder the creation of a highly adaptive culture. You have also explored how a psychologically safe environment fosters a strong learning culture.

By applying the LEASH model, you have incorporated key psychological dynamics that are present in strong-culture environments to systematically drive culture transformation. You did this based on a strong positive emotional culture, taking into consideration identity issues as well.

ACKNOWLEDGE To gain clarity about your firm's cultural gaps, you

- assessed your firm's current culture and gaps related to your future desired state.
- recognized the assumptions about failure and learning within the organization that influence learning and adaptability.

CHALLENGE To question and adapt underlying assumptions that may foster misalignment between current and desired culture, you

- examined and adjusted deeply ingrained beliefs about failure and performance.
- fostered a safe environment where team members feel encouraged to discuss mistakes openly.

TRANSFORM To systemically shape a strong and adaptive culture by incorporating specific psychological dynamics, you

- ensured that positive emotions are prioritized, thus strengthening a positive emotional culture.
- implemented the LEASH model, focusing on leader actions, employee involvement, aligned rewards, stories and signals, and HR alignment.
- consistently developed leadership capabilities to ensure the sustainability of the culture shift.

Shaping culture never ends. It requires sustained effort.
As Satya Nadella wisely observes:

> We're always going to be imperfect. There is always going to be a gap between our espoused culture and the lived experience. To celebrate imperfection is a hard thing.[64]

64 Nadella (2019).

References

Achdiat, I., Mulyani, S., Azis, Y., & Sukmadilaga, C. (2023). Roles of organizational learning culture in promoting innovation. *The Learning Organization, 30*(1), 76–92. https://doi.org/10.1108/TLO-01-2021-0013

Avey, J. B., Avolio, B. J., Crossley, C. D., & Luthans, F. (2009). Psychological ownership: Theoretical extensions, measurement and relation to work outcomes. *Journal of Organizational Behavior, 30*(2), 173–191. https://doi.org/10.1002/job.583

Bandura, A. (1997). *Self-efficacy: The exercise of control.* W. H. Freeman/Times Books/Henry Holt & Co.

Barsade, S., & O'Neill, O. A. (2016). Manage your emotional culture. *Harvard Business Review, 94*(1-2), 58–66.

Brassey, J., De Smet, A., Kothari, A., Lavoie, J., Mugayar-Baldocchi, M., & Zolley, S. (2021, August 2). Future proof. Solving the 'adaptability paradox' for the long term. *McKinsey & Company*. https://www.mckinsey.com/capabilities/people-and-organizational-performance/our-insights/future-proof-solving-the-adaptability-paradox-for-the-long-term

Candelon, F., Krayer, L., Rajendran, S., & Zuluaga Martínez, D. (2023, September 21). How people can create – And destroy – Value with generative AI. *BCG.* https://www.bcg.com/publications/2023/how-people-create-and-destroy-value-with-gen-ai

Chatman, J. A., Caldwell, D. F., O'Reilly, C. A., & Doerr, B. (2014). Parsing organizational culture: How the norm for adaptability influences the relationship between culture consensus and financial performance in high-technology firms. *Journal of Organizational Behavior, 35*(6), 785–808. https://doi.org/10.1002/job.1928

Chen, B.-S., Yuan, C.-H., Yin, B., & Wu, X.-Z. (2021). Positive emotions and entrepreneurial intention: The mediating role of entrepreneurial cognition. *Frontiers in Psychology, 12*, Article 760328. https://doi.org/10.3389/fpsyg.2021.760328

Clark, T. R. (2020). *The 4 stages of psychological safety: Defining the path to inclusion and innovation.* (Kindle version). Berrett-Koehler Publishers.

Daly, J., & Ahmetaj, G. (2020). *Back to the future: Why tomorrow's workforce needs a learning culture*. Emerald Works.

Deloitte USA. (2012). *Core beliefs and culture - Chairman's survey findings*. https://www2.deloitte.com/content/dam/Deloitte/global/Documents/About-Deloitte/gx-core-beliefs-and-culture.pdf

Diener, E., Nickerson, C., Lucas, R. E., & Sandvik, E. (2002). Dispositional affect and job outcomes. *Social Indicators Research, 59*(3), 229–259. https://doi.org/10.1023/A:1019672513984

Edmondson, A. C. (2023). *Right kind of wrong: The science of failing well.* (Kindle version). Simon & Schuster.

Einstein, B. (2025, January 21). Leading successful organizational transformation through culture. *Harvard Business School Online*. https://online.hbs.edu/blog/post/organizational-transformation

Fredrickson, B. L., & Branigan, C. (2005). Positive emotions broaden the scope of attention and thought-action repertoires. *Cognition and Emotion, 19*(3), 313–335.

Garvin, D. A. (1993). Building a learning organization. *Harvard Business Review, 71*(4), 78–91.

Goodrich, N. (2019, March 21). Culture renovation: A blueprint for action. *Institute for Corporate Productivity*. https://www.i4cp.com

Haidt, J. (2000). The positive emotion of elevation. *Prevention & Treatment, 3*(1), Article 3c. https://doi.org/10.1037/1522-3736.3.1.33c

Halmaghi, E.-E., & Todăriță, E.-T. (2023). Creating a learning culture in the organisation. *Scientific Bulletin, 28*(2), 210–214.

Hatfield, E., Cacioppo, J. T., & Rapson, R. L. (1994). *Emotional contagion: Studies in emotion and social interaction*. Cambridge University Press.

Ibarra, H., & Scoular, A. (2019). The leader as coach. How to unleash innovation, energy, and commitment. *Harvard Business Review, 97*(6), 110–119.

Isen, A. M. (1987). Positive affect, cognitive processes, and social behavior. In L. Berkowitz (Ed.), *Advances in experimental social psychology* (Vol. 20, pp. 203–253). Academic Press. https://doi.org/10.1016/S0065-2601(08)60415-3

Jerab, D., & Mabrouk, T. (2023). *The role of leadership in changing organizational culture*. SSRN 4574324.

Joo, B. K., & Shim, J. H. (2010). Psychological empowerment and organizational commitment: The moderating effect of organizational learning culture. *Human Resource Development International, 13*(4), 425–441. https://doi.org/10.1080/13678868.2010.501963

Kets de Vries Institute. (n.d.). Organisational Culture Audit (OCA™). https://kdvi.com/organisational-culture-audit/

Lerner, J. S., & Tetlock, P. E. (1999). Accounting for the effects of accountability. *Psychological Bulletin, 125*(2), 255–275. https://doi.org/10.1037/0033-2909.125.2.255

Martin, A. J. (2004). The role of positive psychology in enhancing satisfaction, motivation, and productivity in the workplace. *Journal of Organizational Behavior Management, 24*(1-2), 113–133. https://doi.org/10.1300/J075v24n01_07

McGuire, J. B., & Palus, C. J. (2018). Vertical transformation of leadership culture. *Integral Review, 14*(1), 144–166.

Nadella, S. (2019, February 14). View from the top. Lecture at Stanford Graduate School of Business [Video]. *YouTube*. https://www.youtube.com/watch?v=rtgN27z0oi0

O'Reilly, C. (2024). How Microsoft transformed its culture: Five levers for organizational cultural change. *Management and Business Review, 4*(1), 41–50, 44. https://doi.org/10.1177/2694105820240401006

O'Reilly, C. A., & Chatman, J. A. (1996). Culture as social control: Corporations, cults, and commitment. In B. M. Staw & L. L. Cummings (Eds.), *Research in organizational behavior: An annual series of analytical essays and critical reviews* (Vol. 18, pp. 157–200). Elsevier Science/JAI Press.

Oswald, A. J., Proto, E., & Sgroi, D. (2015). Happiness and productivity. *Journal of Labor Economics, 33*(4), 789–822. https://doi.org/10.1086/681096

Schein, E. H. (1992). *Organizational culture and leadership*. Jossey-Bass.

Schein, E. H., & Schein, P. A. (2017). *Organizational culture and leadership* (5th ed.). Wiley.

Sekerka, L. E., & Fredrickson, B. L. (2008). Establishing positive emotional climates to advance organizational transformation. In N. M. Ashkanasy & C. L. Cooper (Eds.), *Research companion to emotion in organizations* (pp. 531–545). Edward Elgar.

Senge, P. M. (1990). *The fifths discipline: The art and practice of the learning organization*. Doubleday/Currency.

Simon-Kucher & Partners in collaboration with Bucerius Center on the Legal Profession. (2025). *The AI-Conomics of legal services. How generative AI will transform the commercial model of law*.

Whitley, E. A., Gal, U., & Kjaergaard, A. (2014). Who do you think you are? A review of the complex interplay between information systems, identification, and identity. *European Journal of Information Systems, 23*(1), 17–35. https://doi.org/10.1057/ejis.2013.34

Zhou, H., & Chen, J. (2021). How does psychological empowerment prevent emotional exhaustion? Psychological safety and organizational embeddedness as mediators. *Frontiers in Psychology, 12*. https://doi.org/10.3389/fpsyg.2021.546687

4

Mastering Polarities to Lead Strategic Conversations that Propel Transformation

M. Bernhardt, *Leading Transformation in Law Firms*, Law for Professionals,
https://doi.org/10.1007/978-3-031-98653-6_4

Contents

» The test of a first-rate intelligence is the ability to hold two opposing ideas in mind at the same time and still retain the ability to function.[1]—F. Scott Fitzgerald

Managing this transformation will be Marissa's most ambitious initiative as Managing Partner. With the end of her term already in sight, the outcome of this transformation will define her legacy. Marissa is determined to make it a success. With 23 years of experience in this firm, Marissa knows the firm needs to transform substantially to keep playing at the top of their industry.

Since its inception, the firm has thrived on **internal competition among partners** who took pride in their entrepreneurial spirit and zest for excellence.

However, their approach started **reducing the firm's potential for growth** and its competitive edge. While Marissa's firm was missing out on new market opportunities, more agile competitors were intensifying their collaboration within their partnerships and seized opportunities to expand their business.

? How will Marissa convince her peers that shifting from internal competition to internal collaboration is the best way to ensure and advance the firm's prosperity in the future?

Marissa decides to use the next partner meeting to share her vision for the firm's future and inspire the partners to take part in this transformation.

In the lead-up to the meeting, Marissa feels well-prepared and cautiously optimistic about the outcome. Of course, she anticipates a high likelihood of an intense and controversial discussion, especially since some very high-performing peers may not immediately buy into her initiative. Nonetheless, first and foremost, Marissa is excited about all the opportunities this transformation will bring to everyone in the firm.

Marissa kicks off the meeting with a clear and concise presentation. She shares her analysis and emphasizes the disadvantages of internal competition—particularly the many missed opportunities for expanding and enhancing the business. She then outlines the **advantages of internal collaboration**, such as leveraging their peer network to better meet their clients' rising demand for advice across various legal fields. She reminds her peers of embarrassing incidents where, due to an absence of internal communication, partners from different practice groups had simultaneously pitched for the same client.

Marissa also reminds them of fruitless attempts to install low-barrier cross-selling initiatives, such as cross-practice-group round tables. Those had grandly failed because partners either ignored invitations or failed to attend meetings. She also warns that the competitive mindset between partners has already trickled down to associates who don't share information and insights with their peers either, resent each other's successes, and consider each other as rivals competing for the next career step.

---

1 Fitzgerald (1936), p. 41.

Not stopping there, Marissa cites first-class research demonstrating that partners who collaborate on client acquisition and cross-selling achieve significantly better financial results.[2]

Puzzled, Marissa realizes her presentation has stirred up a hornet's nest. Her peers react agitatedly; some raise their voices. Everyone seems to be talking at the same time, and there is fierce disagreement about whether and how to move forward.

Marissa senses this meeting is slipping from her hands; she barely manages the chaos ensuing from her presentation. The scheduled time for the meeting is up, nothing is solved, and partners start leaving the room to take important client calls.

Reflecting on how the meeting went, Marissa feels stuck, frustrated by her peers' lack of understanding and their intense resistance. Although she has a strong bias for action, she senses that **just pushing harder won't make the transformation come to life**. There has to be a better way.

She recalls a conversation with her good friend Tim, a Managing Partner at a professional services firm, about his firm's past attempt to shift from internal competition to collaboration. She decides to call him for advice.

In the short conversation that follows, Marissa's energy shifts from exhaustion to excitement. Tim offers an idea that changes everything:

Instead of seeing competition and collaboration as mutually exclusive choices, Marissa could think of them as two elements of an interdependent and mutually reinforcing pair. Both elements, **competition, and collaboration, could join forces to bring about transformational change**.

This was a radically different way of thinking about the transformational challenge. Marissa feels a surge of excitement as she envisions leading this transformation with such an integrative approach.

Reassured by the great success of Tim's firm, Marissa is now more determined than ever to embark on the transformational journey and leverage the power of skillfully and sustainably balancing competition and collaboration.

Transformation Strategy: Torn Between Two Competing Choices

? What would you do if you realized that your firm was oscillating between two opposing forces and you had to make a decision?

For example:

- Should you continue prioritizing **short-term benefits** in the partnership's investment decisions, or should you shift toward operating from a **long-term strategic focus**?
- Should you continue to reward partners for their strong focus on client work and **billable hours**, or should you shift toward recognizing those partners who

2 Dixon et al. (2023).

also invest significant time and energy in **developing young talent**, contributing to long-term organizational growth?
- Should you continue to emphasize **risk avoidance** and minimizing uncertainties in decision-making, or should you shift toward encouraging partners to actively explore new opportunities, embracing **experimentation** and learning from mistakes?

The way many senior leaders automatically think about these and similar questions can severely limit the success of transformation efforts.

When faced with what seem like opposing choices, it's easy to fall into the trap of thinking you have to choose one over the other. This often leads to a dynamic where you try to persuade others that your choice is the right one, the best or only way forward. Typically, an ugly tug-of-war follows where everyone ends up in one of two camps: those who advocate for the transformation and those who "resist" forcefully.

At times, you won't even get buy-in to embark on a transformation journey. Thus, the transformation is dead before it even starts. Or you might encounter strong passive resistance during the entire transformation process—people fail to follow through on their commitments, and the transformation slowly dies.

The secret to getting buy-in and successfully leading a transformation in these seemingly "binary" situations is to completely shift your perspective on the challenge at hand. You do not have to choose between two seemingly antagonistic views. Instead, each view is valid, yet each is only partially correct. As Scott F. Fitzgerald so aptly put it, true intelligence lies in holding two opposing ideas at the same time. By **smartly combining both perspectives** instead of favoring one of the other, you will achieve the best transformation outcome.

The capacity to recognize seemingly rivaling perspectives as equally valid and valuable, to maximize both perspectives' advantages while minimizing both perspectives' overuses, is what changes the whole conversation. You will be much more likely to get buy-in from your stakeholders, encounter far less resistance throughout the process, and significantly increase the chances of achieving a sustainable transformation.

ⓘ This ability is also known as **polarity management**, a concept first articulated by Barry Johnson (2005).[3]

It involves skillfully navigating a polarity, where two seemingly contradictory perspectives—or poles—are simultaneously leveraged to drive transformation success.

For you as a senior leader, **knowing how to handle polarities skillfully** is a top skill in our turbulent, fast-paced days.[4]

3 Johnson (2005).
4 Van de Ven and Poole (1988) and Smith and Lewis (2022) (Kindle version).

Polarities tend to surface more strongly in environments characterized by (1) faster change, (2) greater plurality, or (3) more scarcity.[5] In the near future, we will most likely see yet another rise of these conditions.

Research by Johnson shows that **organizations that tap into the power of polarities** have a **significant competitive advantage** and outperform those that don't.[6]

Leveraging this skill will make you a more effective leader because:

- You will successfully initiate a transformation, lead the process, and achieve your goals to transform your firm sustainably.
- You will understand a key—and often hidden—reason why people resist significant change, and you will be able to support them effectively to dissolve that resistance.
- You will solve conflicts between groups that are *"stuck"* and unable to agree on whether a transformation is necessary, what needs to change, and how to do it, ultimately reducing the time required to achieve the envisioned goal.

Leveraging the ACT Process to Master Polarities

There are three steps to effectively leveraging polarities for successful transformation using the ACT process:

The first step (ACKNOWLEDGE) is recognizing that you are dealing with a polarity instead of a problem, which is often easier said than done.

In the second step (CHALLENGE), you question your current mental approach and activate a polarity mindset to unlock opportunities for harnessing the benefits of seemingly opposing perspectives.

The third step (TRANSFORM) focuses on designing concrete, long-term strategies and actions to maximize the advantages of both perspectives while minimizing their downsides.

Acknowledge the Polarity's Distinctive Features

First, it is essential to identify the exact nature of the challenge you are facing, including its specific characteristics and inherent tensions. This requires recognizing the value of opposing perspectives when considering the shift from competition to collaboration.

Distinguish Between Problems and Polarities

The first key question is this:

5 Smith and Lewis (2022) (Kindle version), p. 120 [location 1635].
6 Johnson (2005).

Are you dealing with a problem or a polarity?

A problem is *"a question or puzzle that needs to be solved."*[7] By definition, problems have known solutions we can implement based on existing knowledge. For instance, we can call on an expert who will figure out what to do. Established approaches and current expertise suffice to solve a problem. We often find an adequate solution using an **either/or mindset**, which helps us weigh the pros and cons of different options and make a choice. Indeed, leaders need to be very skilled in activating an either/or mindset to problem-solve.

A polarity, also known as a **paradox**, poses an adaptive challenge—a gap between the current and a desired future state that, unlike problems, cannot be bridged with existing approaches, expertise, or behaviors.

Though a polarity's elements may seem contradictory, it consists of two poles that form a dynamic pair.[8] The two poles reinforce and need each other over time for optimal positive impact.

To effectively navigate polarities, we need to adopt a **both/and mindset**, also referred to as **polarity mindset**.

The simplest **example of a polarity** is *inhaling*—one pole—and *exhaling*—the other pole. When we inhale, we get fresh oxygen. But it seems counterproductive to decide that we will only inhale from now on. The result would be too much carbon dioxide in our system. Thus, we need to exhale to clean out the carbon dioxide. Correspondingly, it would not be wise to only exhale from now on. The result would be a lack of oxygen. We need inhalation **and** exhalation; both require each other for maximum positive effect.

However, when it comes to many other, less obvious polarities, leaders often struggle to manage them effectively. Consider the following polarities:

- preserve stability or embrace change[9]
- focus on short-term investments or focus on long-term investments
- buy or build digital solutions
- exploit current business models or explore options for new business models
- practice law or run a business
- focus on profit or purpose
- focus on profit or care for employees
- foster structured processes or flexible processes
- decentralize or centralize business units
- expand the firm's physical presence or build a strong virtual presence
- compete within teams or collaborate within teams
- compete within the partnership or collaborate within the partnership
- innovate and experiment or stick with the status quo and avoid risks

---

7 Emerson and Lewis (2019) (Kindle Version), p. 9 [location 198].

8 Smith and Lewis (2011), p. 382.

9 For example, a recent study by Miller (2022), p. 74 highlights the difficult balance between stability and change, claiming that *"the legal profession is over-attached to stability and, as a result, forgoes the benefits of change"*.

- convince *"resisters"* of a transformation or sideline *"resisters"*
- reward the individual or reward the team for transforming their behavior (e.g., upskilling)
- promote homogeneous teams or promote diverse teams in the firm
- focus on expectations of *"new"* or *"old"* generations when transforming work conditions.

Reflect and Act

Think about a challenge relevant to a transformation you want to achieve in your firm, and consider whether it might present a polarity challenge:
- What are the two poles, options, or contrasting perspectives?
- What have you tried so far to tackle the challenge?
- How might viewing the challenge as a polarity help?

In Our Scenario Marissa's first realization is that she is not dealing with a problem she can solve with a "yes" to collaboration and a "no" to competition but a polarity that requires her to take a qualitatively different approach to achieve the desired shift.

She understands that the way she had framed the necessary change—from competition toward collaboration—would lead to a back-and-forth discussion with positions becoming increasingly entrenched. She will have to fully recognize the value of both, collaboration and competition.

Assert the Value of Opposing Perspectives

» How wonderful that we have met with a paradox. Now we have some hope of making progress.—Niels Bohr

? How do you get every key stakeholder on board for a transformation?

Instead of pitting people against each other, you want to encourage every stakeholder to hold on to their perspective—along with the associated mindset and behavior—while simultaneously considering the opposing view. You support others to see each perspective and related goals individually while also recognizing their combined strength, just as Niels Bohr so beautifully put it in his quote.

In Our Scenario Marissa asks everyone to list all the benefits and advantages of their preferred perspective. Similarly, partners will collect all potential overuses or downsides that could materialize if people focused solely on their preferred perspective and *"overdid it"*. They do the same for *"the other"* perspective, examining both its benefits and potential pitfalls. Thus, those who advocate for internal competition and those who favor a shift toward internal collaboration will **enumerate the benefits and potential overuses of both perspectives**.

Marissa's role is to challenge everyone to fully consider both perspectives' benefits and overuses, helping partners recognize the inherent value and interdependence of each.

This realization then unlocks a **joint search** for the best ways to combine the benefits and strengths of both perspectives, collaboration and competition.

Table 4.1 illustrates what a resulting collection might look like.

Table 4.1 Benefits and overuses of both perspectives of the polarity [Adapted from Emerson and Lewis (2019) (Kindle Version), p. 28 [location 468]]

BENEFITS - driving excellence by pushing individuals to achieve their best potential - fast processes and decisions (high efficiency) - high individual responsibility and accountability - encourages the growth of individual knowledge and skills - fosters the development of novel approaches and innovative solutions	**BENEFITS** - sharing of expertise and knowledge - creative and innovative solutions thanks to the integration of diverse perspectives - fosters a sense of shared purpose and boosts employee engagement and retention - encourages a culture of continuous learning - enhances client satisfaction through high-value service across different areas of expertise
The Pole of COMPETITION	**The Pole of COLLABORATION**
OVERUSES - lack of information and idea sharing, which limits business revenue - short-term focus on immediate wins and lack of long-term investments - resource hoarding - backstabbing and toxic culture - decline in team morale results in heightened employee turnover	**OVERUSES** - diffusion of responsibility and lack of individual accountability - slower processes and decisions (low efficiency) - having to compromise instead of finding the best solutions - groupthink instead of innovation - communication overload and exhaustion

Reflect and Act

Focus on a transformation challenge you are currently facing.

What are the **benefits and potential downsides of your preferred perspective** (or pole)?

- What are the benefits and positive results of focusing on your preferred pole regarding your clients, employees, the firm's success, and yourself?
- What happens when you focus only on your preferred pole?
- How might this impact your clients, employees, the firm's success, and yourself?

What are the **benefits and potential downsides of the other perspective** (or pole)?

- What are the benefits and positive results when you focus on the other pole regarding your clients, employees, the firm's success, and yourself?
- What happens when you focus solely on the other pole?
- How might this impact your clients, employees, the firm's success, and yourself?

Challenge Automatic Thinking: Shift to a Polarity Mindset

Having recognized the polarity with its inherent tensions, you are now ready to question an either/or mindset and explore how to shift to a both/and mindset. One of Marissa's key tasks is to support her peers in making this shift.

Question Your Automatic Thinking Mode

If you are unaware of its influence, your automatic thinking mode, or mindset, can limit the effectiveness of the transformation.

A mindset is a framework or a lens that helps us interpret experiences[10] and make sense of a complex reality.[11] A defining element of a mindset is the extent to which we are open to new information, willing to challenge our assumptions, and ready to ask open-ended questions to gain new insights.

We will focus on two different mindsets, an either/or mindset and a both/and mindset, also referred to as a polarity mindset or paradox mindset.

When We Operate from an Either/or Mindset[12] we strive to choose between two options by favoring one over the other. We look for right and wrong. Examples are the choice to hire Person A or Person B, to leave our job, or to stay. As a leader, you need to resort to either/or thinking in various challenging situations. Also, in our professional roles, we are trained to think dichotomously. An essential part of many lawyers' professional activity involves making clear distinctions, for example, deciding between right versus wrong, winning or losing, or advocating for one side against another. Their role often requires a strong commitment to their client's position, which can reinforce an either/or mindset. Also, legal education may unintentionally cultivate an either/or mindset: *"Our education and training thus prepare us to advocate only for one side, and, as a result, lawyers are underprepared to realize when opposite values are equally right, mutually necessary, and individually insufficient"*.[13]

10 Dweck (2006).
11 Gupta and Govindarajan (2002).
12 Emerson and Lewis (2019) (Kindle Version), p. 76 [location 1089].
13 Miller (2022), p. 65.

When We Operate from a Both/and Mindset we can hold opposing ideas simultaneously without having to choose between them. We accept the tensions that arise between potentially contradicting ideas. We look for value in both perspectives and strive to harmonize them to capture the benefits of each. We feel energized when we succeed in embracing and integrating conflicting demands.

According to research, the more we actively identify underlying polarities using a both/and mindset, the better we can address them openly, the more others perceive us as innovative and productive, and the higher our job satisfaction.[14]

Empirically, we rarely operate from a both/and mindset. No matter how well educated or trained we are, most of us tend to default to either/or thinking.[15]

? Why is that the case?

First, either/or thinking is fast. Evolutionarily, it helps our predictability-loving brains to decide quickly whether a situation is safe or dangerous. As this was key to our physical survival for a very long time on earth, our brains, by default, see things in opposition—unless we diligently train them to do otherwise.[16]

Second, either/or thinking eliminates the uncertainty and intense emotions that so often accompany polarities: When confronted with a polarity and its inherent tensions, we often experience discomfort due to the perceived lack of clarity and high complexity of the challenge. Often, we don't know how to bring a transformation to life by attending to both perspectives or poles simultaneously. We look for ways to minimize the uncertainty and regain stability by **taking control** of the situation. We do this by choosing between options, if only to regain a sense of control, at least temporarily:

» The easiest way to feel in control when facing paradoxes, at least temporarily, is to make a clear decision between options.[17]

By prematurely making a decision, we fall into a **bias** called "the illusion of control"—a term coined by Ellen Langer in 1975—which leads us to overestimate our competence and ability to control outcomes.[18] This bias inevitably leads to mediocre transformation results, as we leverage only half of the polarity's potency for sustained transformation.

Activate a Polarity Mindset

? How can we get better at activating a both/and mindset and surface the polarity's inherent values?

14 Smith and Lewis (2022) (Kindle version), p. 122 [location 1669].
15 Emerson and Lewis (2019) (Kindle Version), p. 17 [location 321].
16 Emerson and Lewis (2019) (Kindle Version), p. 18 [location 333].
17 Smith and Lewis (2022) (Kindle version), p. 145 [location 2027].
18 Smith and Lewis (2022) (Kindle version), p. 145 [location 2027].

Fig. 4.1 Rubin's face-vase illusion [Sebasgiu (n.d.)]

Take a look at Fig. 4.1—What do you see?

Did you at first see a goblet? That is undoubtedly an accurate observation.

Did you at first see two faces? That, too, is undoubtedly an accurate observation.

This optical illusion, developed by Danish psychologist Edgar Rubin, plays with the relationship between foreground and background. Often, we have difficulty seeing both figures at the same time. When we focus on just one element—the goblet or the faces—we can lure ourselves into believing our lopsided perception to be correct and complete. But while both views—the goblet or the faces—are equally valid, neither is complete.

The same is true for polarities: while both views—in Marissa's case, either a preference for collaboration or competition—are equally valid and accurate, none of them paints the whole picture. Seeing and understanding the "opposite" perspective becomes possible when we temporarily let go of our preferred view.

In Rubin's optical illusion, this happens when we swiftly shift our focus between the goblet and the faces. In essence, this ambiguous figure illustrates the potential to activate a both/and mindset, moving from "being either right or wrong" to "being right and being right."

? What is the secret to shifting to a both/and mindset?

To get there, we need to start **asking different questions**, such as:

- How else could I look at this image (or this situation)?
- What am I not seeing yet?
- How might someone else describe this image (or this situation)?
- What other questions could I ask to better understand this image (or this situation)?

To be able to ask these questions, you first need to THINK of them. And you will only think of them if you are genuinely **open to new insights**, willing to consider that you might be missing something and **curious** to find out what that is.

Unfortunately, we are often least curious when we should be most. Instead, we defend our perspective by zooming in on incomplete information while arbitrarily ignoring other information that may be equally important. We do this in the hope of validating our perspective. According to Miron-Spektor et al. (2018), the more pronounced our polarity mindset is, the greater our ability to accept a polarity's tensions as natural and valuable,[19] and to embrace the emotions that often accompany them.

Curiosity, asking questions that broaden our perspective, and openness to new insights are all essential to our ability to operate from a both/and perspective when facing a challenge.

Of course, effectively shifting our thinking from either/or to both/and is not a one-time effort. We need to continuously activate a both/and mindset to override our, often automatic, attraction toward either/or thinking.[20] Growth comes with consistent practice.

Reflect and Act

- How curious are you when facing opposition to your perspective?
- How open are you to understanding someone with an opposing opinion?
- How easily can you ask open-ended questions to learn something new and better understand a perspective that differs significantly from yours?
- How often do you ask questions to listen in? And how often do you ask questions to respond?
- When is your next opportunity to practice curiosity, openness to new insights, open-ended questions, and active listening to shift from either/or to both/and thinking?

A polarity mindset helps you surface the underlying values behind both poles—values that fuel the tension between them. It also enables you to unlock both poles' combined transformative capacity.

How? Even though you may cognitively embrace the idea of valuing and leveraging both poles to achieve a sustainable transformation, concerns and fears can still get in the way.

For example, considering yourself to be competitive, ambitious, success-driven, fast, and decisive in your actions, you might fear losing that part of your identity by integrating the pole of collaboration more into your thinking and behavior. You may fear excessive collaboration—the *"other"* pole's overuse—diminishing the benefits of your preferred pole.

19 Miron-Spektor et al. (2018).
20 Peters (2011).

In this sense, displayed resistance vis-à-vis the other pole is always highly valuable information. **Those who strongly *"resist"* one perspective (or pole) are concerned that their values might be compromised**.

Asking thoughtful questions to uncover the values inherent in each perspective helps everyone recognize the core values of each pole. This shifts the discussion toward embracing both perspectives and exploring ways to bring their joint benefits and strengths to life in the transformation.

Reflect and Act

Think about your concerns regarding leveraging the benefits of both poles in a specific situation:
- What feels risky about balancing both poles?
- What is your assumed worst-case scenario?
- What aspect of your professional identity or core values would need to shift or expand for you to effectively navigate both poles?

Revealing the core values of each perspective, along with deeper concerns and fears, makes it much easier to focus on leveraging the benefits of both while ensuring the core values are protected.

At this point, you will typically fully embrace the paradox that, **to gain more of the benefits of your preferred pole, you must incorporate the other pole to some extent**, allowing its benefits to counterbalance the overuses of your preferred pole.

Reflect and Act

Consider what it would be like if you could integrate the joint benefits of both poles:
- What becomes possible by harmonizing both poles—their respective strengths and advantages? Be specific and visualize concrete business situations where these strengths would make a positive difference.
- What positive transformation outcomes could you achieve for your firm?

Transform the Strategic Conversation: Activate the Polarity's Strength

We challenged a default either/or mindset and discussed options to shift to a both/and mindset. We surfaced core values that fuel each perspective and searched for opportunities to combine the benefits of both perspectives while preserving their core values.

Now, it is time to activate the poles' combined strengths.

Harness the Polarity's Benefits While Preventing Overuses

Our goal is to maximize both perspectives' advantages while ensuring we minimize overuses as much as possible.

A structured inquiry is a powerful way to help you create a roadmap for sustainably harnessing the upsides of both poles simultaneously.

One effective approach is to use a **cascading question, carefully dissected into three parts**.

To explore this in practice, let's return to Marissa and her discussion with her peers:

First, Marissa and her peers look at the benefits of collaboration which currently abounds. They ask:

"How can we gain more of the benefits of collaboration?"

They brainstorm—both individually and collectively—potential strategies and concrete actions while keeping relevant values and concerns in mind.

Second, they move to the benefits of competition, the currently dominant pole. They build on the first part of the question:

"How can we gain more of the benefits of collaboration **without losing the benefits of competition** (e.g. without sacrificing our speed and strong entrepreneurial spirit)?"

During this brainstorming session on potential strategies and actions, it is essential to capture the concerns raised by partners.

Third, Marissa and her peers complete the cascading question with its final part:

"How can we gain more of the benefits of collaboration without losing the benefits of competition—**so that we can best serve our clients through entrepreneurial thinking and a strong internal sharing of information and knowledge, ultimately enhancing growth?"**

Throughout the inquiry, the following **additional questions** help the group consider how they will evaluate the strategies and actions and measure their impact. Everyone needs to know how to hold each other accountable for their actions:

"What would a courageous action look like?"

"What do we need to start/stop/continue doing?"

These are some ideas the group might come up with:

- bring practice groups together to share leads and ideas regularly
- explore the possibility of setting shared targets across practice groups
- organize innovation challenges that require collaboration between different practice groups

- develop performance metrics that account for both individual and team/practice group contributions
- invest in training programs that enhance both individual skills and teamwork abilities
- equip employees and leaders with tools to address conflict constructively
- make discussions on balancing competition and collaboration a regular agenda item in partnership meetings.

4

The transformation goal has now become clear, as well as concrete actions to achieve it.

Rather than saying, *"Let's move from competition toward collaboration"*, the partnership can commit to the following statement: "*We are going to do X (Collaboration) while preserving the benefits of Y (Competition).*"

Monitor and Adapt Strategies to Keep the Balance

You have now laid out a spectrum of beneficial behaviors and mindsets to successfully shift toward greater collaboration without losing the benefits of competition.

The partnership can now **prioritize strategies and actions** based on their impact, feasibility, and effort.

To ensure clarity and alignment, the partnership will specify who needs to do what and when. Finally, it needs to establish an **accountability process** to heighten the probability that everyone will follow through on the agreed agenda.

Since not every action will be effective, partners need a process that allows them to refine strategies while letting go of those that have little or negative impact. To facilitate this, it is helpful to define small action steps that serve as **experiments** whose outcomes will be carefully **evaluated against the transformation goal**. This goal remains clear: to enhance collaboration without sacrificing the benefits of competition.

Additionally, it is essential to install a **monitoring process**.

Questions that might help the group develop an effective process include, for example:

- How will we quickly recognize when the overuses of one pole—collaboration or competition—are materializing, so that we can take countermeasures?
- What process will we establish to systematically evaluate the results of our current strategy and determine whether both poles remain balanced or if different strategies are needed?
- What communication system should be in place to help us quickly identify and address the downsides of either pole when they arise?

◘ Table 4.2 illustrates how you can visualize the results of the process, including specific strategies to leverage the benefits of both poles, as well as a monitoring system that provides early warnings in case one of both poles are overemphasized.

During the transformation toward greater collaboration, whenever Marissa communicates the transformation's goal, she will naturally avoid a typical trap that

Table 4.2 Overview of key elements to smartly navigate a polarity [Adapted version of the *"Polarity Navigator"*, developed by Johnson (1992) and Emerson and Lewis (2019) (Kindle Version), p. 54 [location 796]]

Strategies to foster benefits of competition	**BENEFITS** - driving excellence & individual growth - high efficiency - high individual accountability	**BENEFITS** - expertise and knowledge sharing - creative solutions - high retention	**Strategies to foster benefits of collaboration**
	The Pole of COMPETITION	**The Pole of COLLABORATION**	
Monitoring and rapid alert system for overuse of competition	**OVERUSES** - no idea sharing - short-term focus - toxic culture, high turnover	**OVERUSES** - no individual accountability - low efficiency - communication overload	**Monitoring and rapid alert system for overuse of collaboration**

change communication is prey to. Often, change is communicated by focusing on one pole as the problem, the other pole being the solution: The messenger outlines the problem, highlights the overuses currently emerging, and presents a plan to achieve the benefits of the opposite pole. The proclaimed transformational goal sounds like this: *"We want to move away from competition and will start to foster collaboration."*

This message is likely to increase resistance, at least among some leaders in the firm.

As discussed, a more appropriate key message throughout the transformation is this: "*We are going to do X (Collaboration) while preserving the benefits of Y (Competition)*".

This balanced message must be repeated consistently to sustain and strengthen buy-in for the transformation goal.

Reflect and Act

- What strategies and actions could help you transform your firm by leveraging the benefits of both poles?
- How can you maximize the benefits of the currently dominant pole (e.g., long-term focus in business decisions, cross-practice-group collaboration, aligned leadership culture, clear purpose) without losing the advantages of the other pole?
- What do you need to start, continue, or stop doing?
- How can you monitor progress and adjust if some actions do not yield the intended results?

Summary

Together with your fellow partners, you have created a transformation strategy that balances the pole of collaboration with the pole of competition in a way that allows you to harness the advantages of increased collaboration without losing the benefits of competition. Using this balanced process, you got the entire partnership on board for this significant shift. Thus, it is likely you will achieve sustainable transformation.

ACKNOWLEDGE To more deeply understand the quality of the situation you are dealing with, you

- recognized the fact that you are confronting a polarity rather than a problem.
- valued the polarity's multiple benefits and potential overuses as essential elements to consider and balance to achieve transformation.

CHALLENGE To find a balanced way to deal with the polarity, you

- challenged an *"either/or"* mindset and activated a *"both/and"* mindset.
- identified core values to preserve when combining the benefits of both poles for a sustainable transformation.

TRANSFORM To harness the benefits of both perspectives while making sure their downsides don't materialize, you

- discussed and decided on concrete strategies and actions to balance both poles.
- installed a monitoring process to measure progress toward the transformation goal and adjust strategies and actions if needed.

Leaders in professional services firms will increasingly need to navigate a growing number of polarities in the future.

As Smith and Lewis (2022) highlight, three conditions make underlying polarities more salient:[21]

▪ Faster Change

As the pace of change accelerates with no end in sight—creating unpredictable conditions and growing uncertainty—tensions between seemingly contradictory perspectives intensify. Leaders feel pressured to make faster choices. The urgency to act can lead to binary either/or thinking, rather than carefully balancing competing perspectives.

---

21 Smith and Lewis (2022) (Kindle version), p. 120 [location 1635].

- **Greater Plurality**

The more perspectives, stakeholders, and interests exist within an organization and in the organization's environment, the more conflicting goals, roles, and values emerge. This often creates a strong impulse to take sides rather than embrace integration.

- **Increased Scarcity**

When resources become more limited—whether time, budget, or talent—the pressure to make either/or decisions grows. Leaders may feel compelled to prioritize one group over another rather than finding solutions that balance competing needs over time.

Leaders who operate from a both/and mindset—resisting the urge to default to either/or choices—are far more likely to lead transformation successfully.

Strengthening your polarity mindset will be essential for leading your firm into the future effectively.

Figure 4.2 offers a comprehensive illustration of how to skillfully handle polarities.

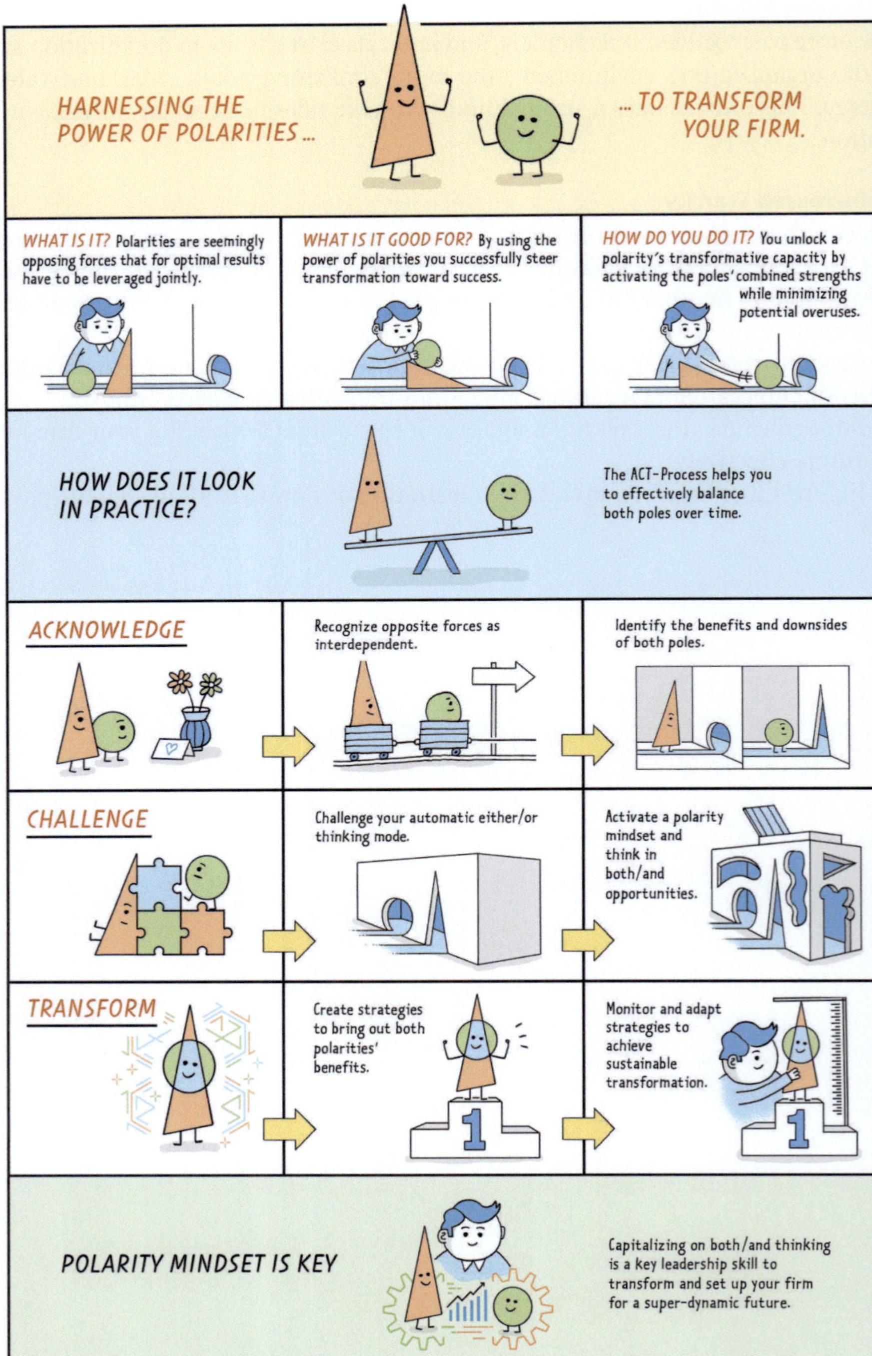

Fig. 4.2 Harnessing the power of polarities (illustration: Stephan Katz)

References

Dixon, M., McKenna, T., Channer, R., & Freeman, K. (2023, November-December). What today's rainmakers do differently. Business development at professional services firms is outdated. Here's what works now. *Harvard Business Review*.

Dweck, C. S. (2006). *Mindset: The new psychology of success*. Random House.

Emerson, B., & Lewis, K. (2019). *Navigating polarities: Using both/and thinking to lead transformation*. (Kindle Version). Paradoxical Press.

Fitzgerald, F. S. (1936, February). The crack-up. *Esquire*, p. 41. Retrieved February 12, 2025, from https://classic.esquire.com/article/share/97a6b0a8-ba1c-4b7b-aa64-0d08dd9fb952

Gupta, A. K., & Govindarajan, V. (2002). Cultivating a global mindset. *The Academy of Management Executive, 16*(1), 116–126. https://doi.org/10.5465/ame.2002.6640211

Johnson, B. (1992). *Polarity management: Identifying and managing unsolvable problems*. HRD Press.

Johnson, B. (2005). *Polarity management: A summary introduction*. Polarity Management Associates. https://rise-leaders.com/wp-content/uploads/2019/07/Polarity-Management-Summary-Introduction.pdf

Miller, B. A. (2022). BOTH: The legal profession's struggle to leverage stability and change. *Harvard Negotiation Law Review, 28*(1), 65–86. https://doi.org/10.2139/ssrn.4101234

Miron-Spektor, E., Ingram, A., Keller, J., Smith, W. K., & Lewis, M. W. (2018). Microfoundations of organizational paradox: The problem is how we think about the problem. *Academy of Management Journal, 61*(1), 26–45. https://doi.org/10.5465/amj.2016.0594

Peters, D. (2011, February 24–25). *Understanding why lawyers resist mediation* [Keynote address]. 2nd Asian Mediation Association Conference: Rediscovering Mediation in the 21st Century, Kuala Lumpur, Malaysia.

Sebasgiu. (n.d.). Rubin's vase [Illustration]. *Wikimedia Commons*. https://commons.wikimedia.org/w/index.php?curid=121487552

Smith, W., & Lewis, M. (2022). *Both/and thinking: Embracing creative tensions to solve your toughest problems*. (Kindle version). Harvard Business Review Press.

Smith, W. K., & Lewis, M. W. (2011). Toward a theory of paradox: A dynamic equilibrium model of organizing. *Academy of Management Review, 36*(2), 381–403. https://doi.org/10.5465/amr.2011.59330958

Van de Ven, A., & Poole, M. S. (1988). Paradoxical requirements for a theory of change. In R. E. Quinn & K. S. Cameron (Eds.), *Paradox and transformation: Toward a theory of change in organization and management*. Ballinger.

Team Level

Contents

Fostering Psychological Safety to Unlock Team Performance

Contents

M. Bernhardt, *Leading Transformation in Law Firms*, Law for Professionals,
https://doi.org/10.1007/978-3-031-98653-6_5

> For organizations to weather the storms ahead, they need to leverage … the full set of talents and insights available in their workforce. Psychological safety … is what enables employees to use their voices, and it's more important than ever that leaders build it.[1]

Do people in your firm
- share their thoughts, ideas, concerns, and critical feedback openly?
- feel safe to disagree without fear of retribution?
- come up with innovative ideas frequently?
- admit their mistakes and learn from them?

If you can confidently answer *"yes"* to these questions, you have likely created a psychologically safe environment, which is foundational for successful transformation. As Hadley et al. (2023) so clearly stated: Leaders must build psychological safety so employees can fully contribute, especially in uncertain times.

Psychological Safety: Why Top Teams Excel During Transformation

Psychological safety is the belief that the work environment is safe for interpersonal risk-taking: You are convinced that you can interact with your team without fear of being excluded, embarrassed, or punished. You feel that you are allowed and encouraged to voice your ideas, concerns, questions, and critical feedback, and to admit your mistakes, all without fear of negative consequences.[2]

Research shows that *"psychological safety is consistently one of the strongest predictors of team performance, productivity, quality, safety, creativity, and innovation."*[3]

In particular, psychological safety:
- **fosters experimentation, innovation, and creativity**: When employees feel psychologically safe, they are more likely to share innovative ideas and take risks without fear of negative consequences. For example, a study of 328 team members found a positive correlation between psychological safety and creativity.[4]
- **improves team collaboration**: When employees trust they can share their thoughts without fear of judgment, teams are more likely to collaborate effectively, leveraging diverse perspectives to drive transformation forward.
- **enhances effective problem-solving**: When team members speak up about potential issues and obstacles early in a transformation, they often identify challenges before they become difficult to address.

1 Hadley et al. (2023).
2 Edmondson (1999).
3 McKinsey & Company (2023).
4 Wang et al. (2018).

- **promotes learning and development:** People feel comfortable seeking and providing honest, respectful feedback and learning from mistakes, which is essential for personal growth and the firm's growth during transformational periods.
- **boosts adaptability**: In psychologically safe environments, people are better equipped to handle the uncertainties of transformation because they trust that they will receive the support needed to develop required capabilities.
- **improves people's ownership and commitment to their work**: When people recognize that their voice matters and they can make a positive impact, they invest more discretionary effort to achieve positive outcomes.
- **fosters productivity**: Research showed that psychological safety boosts productivity by 12%.[5]
- **improves retention**: Also, findings suggest that companies that foster psychological safety have a 27% lower employee turnover.[6]

For more than 25 years, Prof. Amy C. Edmondson of Harvard Business School has researched the impact of psychological safety on **team performance and organizational effectiveness.**[7] Since then, many companies have discovered the power of psychological safety. In 2012, Google launched "Project Aristotle" and studied hundreds of Google's teams to find out why some were unsuccessful while others were remarkably high-performing.[8] After careful analysis, the project found *"that IQ points and money don't necessarily produce results … In fact, the company landed on psychological safety as the single most important factor in explaining high performance."*[9]

Fostering psychological safety is essential for gaining a competitive edge. Firms develop and learn faster when people speak up with their ideas, questions, and critical feedback and when they feel safe admitting mistakes.

When psychological safety is low, **top talent** often leaves for better opportunities elsewhere. In law firms, talent is the most valuable resource. Losing top talent weakens any transformation effort, simply because you lack the very people who could make it a success.

Psychological safety becomes even more crucial in unstable, uncertain, and **unpredictable times**—when law firms must adapt and transform on multiple fronts. **During a transformation, you need teams that perform at their best**, learn quickly, collaborate seamlessly, and leverage their creativity to drive the firm's development.

---

5 Herway (2017).
6 Herway (2017).
7 Edmondson (1999).
8 Duhigg (2016).
9 Clark (2020) (Kindle version), p. 26 [location 292].

Safe and Uncomfortable: The Power of the Learning Zone

When I discuss psychological safety with leaders, often someone says: *"We have that. We don't shout at people. We consider ourselves to be the nice guys."*

But psychological safety doesn't mean being nice to each other, regardless of performance.

On the contrary, **psychological safety goes hand in hand with high-performance standards,**[10] which are especially critical during a transformation.

Both, high psychological safety and high-performance standards are like two sides of the same coin: You foster psychological safety while clearly defining what you expect from others, what they are responsible for, and what they will be held accountable for.

Edmondson distinguishes between four zones[11] of varying levels of psychological safety:

■■ The Apathy Zone

Low psychological safety and low-performance standards

In this zone, teams have little motivation to contribute. Team members disengage and focus on doing their job by the book. They invest their skills, effort, and persistence outside work. In consequence, innovation stagnates, performance plummets, and a culture of mediocrity and passivity evolves over time. When people live in the Apathy Zone, you cannot expect great things from them. Your competitors will pass you by as your firm stands still.

■■ The Comfort Zone

High psychological safety, but low-performance standards

In this zone, typically, teams have a good time working together. They like each other and collaborate well. Performance may be steady but not excellent, as people and teams are not held accountable for their actions. Teams don't improve as much as they could because no one challenges them to stretch beyond their current limits. Complacency can result from people staying in the Comfort Zone for too long. During transformation, when people often need to stretch themselves significantly, teams may resist doing so, resulting in slower and more limited progress.

■■ The Anxiety Zone

Low psychological safety, but high-performance standards

People are held accountable for what they do. However, as psychological safety is low, people constantly try to protect themselves. They are reluctant to share questions, concerns, and critical feedback due to fear of being dressed down. The enormous pressure in the Anxiety Zone creates an environment of constant stress. This stifles creativity, innovation, and collaboration. The culture becomes either

10 Edmondson (2023) (Kindle version), p. 40 [location 611].
11 Edmondson (2018) (Kindle version) [location 778].

unhealthy or outright toxic. During transformations, people try to reduce the risk of appearing incompetent. Thus, transformation falls victim to fear.

The Learning Zone

High psychological safety and high-performance standards

With both psychological safety and performance standards held high, people are committed to the cause. They want to contribute and achieve great results. Feeling safe to voice their ideas, thoughts, questions, and concerns enables them to engage in conversations that lead to innovative solutions. Simultaneously, a strong sense of accountability drives high performance and continuous learning. This balance between high psychological safety and high-performance standards leads to a dynamic and thriving work environment where individuals and the firm excel. During transformation, people know they can take the risk to speak their minds and be candid with colleagues, employees, and superiors. Because people admit and share their mistakes early, the adverse effects can be mitigated.

Reflect and Act

Think of a team you are currently working with on a transformation you aim to achieve:

- In which zone(s) would you place your team?
- What needs to happen for your team to unlock their full potential and enter their *"learning zone"*?

Leveraging the ACT Process to Foster Psychological Safety

? How can you create a psychologically safe environment, enabling teams to fully engage in transformation?

In the first step of the process (ACKNOWLEDGE), you assess the current level of psychological safety in your team. You distinguish four levels of psychological safety and diagnose what level(s) you want to improve.

In the second step (CHALLENGE), you question your team's current level of psychological safety. You help the team understand how psychological safety impacts performance. Together, you co-create an action plan to implement necessary changes that foster psychological safety.

Finally, in the third step (TRANSFORM), you strengthen psychological safety in two ways: You harmonize your firm's internal systems and processes to eliminate factors hindering psychological safety. This alignment helps establish a culture of psychological safety, which is a foundation for any successful transformation. You consistently emphasize the importance of psychological safety to reinforce that it is not a one-time achievement but must be nurtured continuously.

Acknowledge Your Team's Current Level of Psychological Safety

Consider the following **scenario**:

As a Co-Managing Partner, you—together with your fellow Co-Managing Partner, three equity partners from the partner committee, the COO, and CHRO—form a dedicated transformation team leading the firm's shift from a "client first" to a "people first" imperative.

In the past, when a client matter seemed urgent, leaders tended to ask their teams to "go the extra mile", sacrificing weekends and previously agreed-upon working hours. As one mile led to another, over the last few years, your firm has lost a significant number of highly talented employees, with departures steadily rising.

Exit interviews paint a clear picture: Your "client first" approach has consistently placed employees second, and they are drawing their conclusions. If this pattern continues, the firm won't be able to sustain its growth ambitions—simply because there won't be enough qualified people to do the work.

Lately, you have noticed a troubling dynamic in your leadership team responsible for the initiative. You and the CHRO tend to dominate discussions, while two colleagues from the partner committee and the COO rarely voice their thoughts, gradually disengaging. You know you need full commitment from everyone at the table. Right now, you don't know what some members of your leadership team truly think or whether they have fully bought into the transformation effort.

The success of this transformation is at stake.

How to Distinguish the Four Stages of Psychological Safety

According to Timothy Clark's research, there are **four stages of psychological safety**[12] which reflect a natural progression in team interactions. They naturally build on one another, independently from cultural differences:

- **Stage 1: Inclusion Safety**

Inclusion safety satisfies the human desire to connect and belong to others. When there is a high level of inclusion safety, every team member feels a true sense of belonging and unconditional acceptance as part of the team.

This is the precondition for stepping out of comfort zones, taking on more responsibility, and engaging in continuous learning.

Thus, inclusion safety is the foundation for the next three stages.

You may think, *"Well, isn't this a given? Of course, I treat everyone as a human being worthy of my respect independently from their performance, experience, background, or status."*

In practice, despite best intentions, this is what often happens:

12 Clark (2020).

- We tend to grant **"conditional" inclusion safety** only. We assume that a person belongs to our team as long as they perform well. When their performance declines, we subconsciously revoke inclusion: we forget to inform them about developments, exclude them from emails they should be copied on, or overlook them in discussions. Many subtle, often non-verbal signals make it clear to the person that they are no longer included.
- We are often unaware of how we subtly **switch between granting and revoking inclusion safety** to someone. This inconsistency is particularly painful for the person affected because they never know where they stand. Today, they may feel accepted; tomorrow, they may not.

The human desire and need to belong are among the strongest we know. When it is harmed, rebuilding can be difficult: *"A sense of belonging is easy to destroy and hard to build."*[13]

When you successfully establish consistent inclusion safety, you have built the basis for the subsequent stages of psychological safety.

Reflect and Act

Consider the level of inclusion safety in a team you lead that is currently navigating a significant shift or transformation:

- How do you demonstrate that you value each team member as part of the group, regardless of their background, experience, or other attributes?
- How do you encourage open communication and participation from everyone, including quieter team members?
- What biases or stereotypes—whether in yourself or others—might have prevented someone from being unconditionally included in the team?

▪ Stage 2: Learner Safety

Effective learning is the ultimate competitive advantage in any law firm: *"Learners who feel safe are far more willing to practice at the edge of their expertise to experiment, solve difficult problems, and to reflect on their performance."*[14]

When learner safety is high, every team member feels safe to engage in learning—asking questions, sharing thoughts and ideas, and giving and receiving feedback. They do so without fear of being embarrassed, ridiculed, marginalized, or ignored:

When you experience learner safety, you trust that others will not hold your mistakes against you but support and encourage you in the learning process.

Conversely, if you assess the risk and decide that speaking up is too risky, you will start self-censoring and stay silent during important meetings.

In fact, the greatest risk your firm can take is to stop learning.

13 Coyle (2018), p. 22.
14 Clark (2020) (Kindle version), p. 83 [location 1067].

Reflect and Act

Consider the level of learner safety in a team you lead that is currently navigating a significant shift or transformation:

- How do you respond when team members ask questions, seek clarification, or admit mistakes?
- What mechanisms have you put in place to facilitate feedback and continuous learning?
- Can you recall someone in your life—a teacher, mentor, or superior—who created a strong sense of learner safety for you? How did that influence you?

Stage 3: Contributor Safety

With high contributor safety, you feel allowed and invited to contribute to the team, use your skills, and make a positive difference. In this third stage, team members typically experience a higher degree of autonomy and corresponding level of responsibility and accountability than in the first two stages.

In contrast to inclusion and learner safety, contributor safety is based on a condition: You provide someone the opportunity to contribute because they have demonstrated they can deliver—they are prepared, ready, and willing to perform. If the team member does not perform as expected, you might withdraw contributor safety and grant them learner safety instead.

Often, leaders in law firms extend broad invitations for people to contribute, hoping this will be enough to encourage participation. However, this alone isn't enough to spark people's contributions. Instead, you must be explicit about fostering contributor safety. And there is a reason for this: *"Even if you have town halls, listening tours, Slack channels, and culture surveys, it still takes effort and follow-up to ensure that they're working. Otherwise, you're at risk of missing important aspects of what's happening, or of hearing from only those employees who are especially passionate about an issue."*[15]

Reflect and Act

Consider the level of contributor safety in a team you lead that is currently navigating a significant shift or transformation:

- How do you ensure team members feel empowered to contribute their ideas without fear of being dismissed?
- How do you create opportunities for all team members to take on challenging work and make decisions within their areas of responsibility?
- How do you ensure that all team members have equal access to the resources and opportunities needed to contribute effectively?

15 Hadley et al. (2023).

Stage 4: Challenger Safety

Challenger safety is the culminating stage and crucial to driving innovation and transformation. It allows you to challenge the status quo freely—an essential condition for innovation. You believe you can speak up when you see an opportunity to improve things and know you can disagree productively. You are ready to curiously question and challenge the running system of an organization or an element of its cultural DNA. You know that you can openly scrutinize a decision by asking questions such as:

- Why do we choose this path?
- Might there be another, even better option?
- Can I suggest a different way?

At this stage, your personal risk and vulnerability are at their highest because you are *"asking your people to expose themselves to criticism, risk failure, take chances, be vulnerable, not fit in, and feel pain. And you're asking them to do all of this without any real control of the outcome."*[16]

Challenger safety is essential for innovation. One reason lies in the distinction between defensive and offensive innovation.[17]

Defensive innovation is a response to an external challenge. It occurs when a stakeholder, such as a client, tells you they want something different from you, and you must figure out how to deliver that. The same occurs when a new competitor or technology emerges. You don't have to challenge the status quo internally; someone else outside of the firm is already doing it. Thus, *"defensive innovation is change choosing you."*[18]

Offensive innovation, in contrast, *"is you choosing change."*[19] It is a response to an opportunity. Offensive, proactive innovation typically involves a significantly higher personal risk of being exposed, ridiculed, or ignored as you dare question something that has never been questioned before.

Thus, when you are granted contributor safety, you will contribute to defensive innovation but not necessarily to offensive, proactive innovation. For this to happen, you also need to experience challenger safety.

ⓘ In any transformation effort, challenger safety is absolutely essential.

Without it, your team won't be as innovative as you would like because people don't feel free to challenge a course of action. But you need to know what people think, what concerns they have, and what they see as risky or unwise—at any point during a transformation.

16 Clark (2020) (Kindle version), p. 137 [location 1783].
17 Clark (2020) (Kindle version), p. 100 [location 1287].
18 Clark (2020) (Kindle version), p. 100 [location 1287].
19 Clark (2020) (Kindle version), p. 100 [location 1287].

Reflect and Act

Consider the level of challenger safety in a team you lead that is currently navigating a significant shift or transformation:

- When was the last time you challenged the status quo?
- How do you respond to feedback or ideas that challenge your views or the established way of doing things?
- How do you handle conflicts or disagreements within the team?

Measure Psychological Safety in Your Team

? What options do you have to assess the current level of your team's psychological safety to learn more about the status quo?

There are a variety of **diagnostic tools** your team can use to this effect:

The "Team Psychological Safety Survey", developed by Prof. Amy C. Edmondson, provides valuable and valid insights through a Psychological Safety Index.[20] Another option is the "Four Stages Team Survey"[21] which determines red zones (low psychological safety), blue zones (high psychological safety), and neutral zones (mixed levels of psychological safety). The latter gives you an overall score of psychological safety for your team.

The survey results will form the basis for the next step—a team discussion on psychological safety—highlighting areas that need improvement to ensure full engagement of every team member in the transformation.

Challenge the Status Quo of Psychological Safety in Your Team

To better understand the reasons behind the survey results, you discuss them with your team. Together, you decide how the level of psychological safety can be improved.

Explore the Root Causes of Your Team's Psychological Safety Level

At this point, your team has completed the survey and received the results.

Next, you dive deeper into the specific results and suggestions in the survey, allowing everyone to familiarize themselves with the concept and impact of psychological safety in the context of the attempted transformation.

20 The Fearless Organization Scan (n.d.).
21 LeaderFactor (n.d.).

You can lead and facilitate the conversation yourself or choose an internal or external facilitator to steer the conversation. When discussing the influence of psychological safety with the team, make sure to ask team members for as many practical examples and observations as possible.

In Our Scenario your leadership team discovers it is doing pretty well in the first three stages of psychological safety. However, the fourth stage, namely challenger safety, is an issue for some team members. The survey flagged it as a red zone, which is particularly problematic in the current effort to shift the firm's strategic focus from "clients first" to "people first". Some team members feel they cannot be candid about their thoughts on the envisioned change. They believe they are not allowed to scrutinize whether the chosen path is the right one or suggest alternative courses of action.

In the conversation with your leadership team, you realize that you are not providing sufficient challenger safety. While you encourage fellow leaders to challenge your proposed strategy, in practice, whenever someone dares to do just that, you respond with a lengthy explanation of why your approach is the only correct way forward. Many thought-terminating clichés, including statements like "research clearly shows", follows, and the discussion comes to a halt. Your fellow partners and the COO struggle to engage in a constructive debate because your (seemingly) rational arguments make it difficult, and they hesitate to challenge you to avoid being seen as innovation-blockers. At the same time, they don't feel comfortable moving forward without having had a chance to freely express their differing perspectives. As a result, they disengage from discussions, keeping their perspectives out of the conversation. You, your fellow Co-Managing Partner, and the CHRO were unaware of this detrimental pattern. From now on, your role is to listen with intent rather than immediately reacting when others challenge your preferred course of action.

By the end of the conversation, it has become clear that challenger safety must be improved.

Co-create an Action Plan to Elevate Team Psychological Safety

Now that you have agreed on putting effort into augmenting the level of challenger safety in the team, you will have to co-create an action plan to achieve that. It entails concrete advice for how to improve psychological safety through specific behaviors.

An action plan should cover concrete **behavioral suggestions** for team members and leaders to foster psychological safety.

In Our Scenario your leadership team would agree on specific behaviors that help strengthen challenger safety. ◘ Table **5.1** presents helpful agreements.

In addition to concrete behaviors, an action plan should identify which internal **structures and systems** can help foster psychological safety.

For example, the **performance management** system plays a crucial role. As Amy C. Edmondson provocatively asks:

» Are teams being celebrated for having honest conversations that catch errors early, involve healthy forms of conflict, and generate feelings of inclusion? If you're not sure, then this is a good time to reassess your performance management system. Alignment between what you ask of employees and what you reward is critical for engagement and holds both sides accountable.[22]

Table 5.2 illustrates what an action plan might look like in practice.

Table 5.1 Key behaviors that improve challenger safety in your team

Call out defensive behavior As you have realized that you tend to react quickly, strongly, and defensively to anyone challenging your idea for the strategic shift, you ask your peers to immediately call out defensive behavior as soon as they notice it. Doing so fosters open conversations on how to respond more constructively to differing thoughts and comments.
Control and regulate non-verbal cues You commit to paying close attention to your immediate non-verbal reactions: Do you signal discomfort when your ideas are challenged? Instead, choose openness and gratitude as your initial response when others question your ideas. When you notice others reacting inappropriately to feedback on their ideas, emphasize the importance of a high tolerance for candor.
Implement a no-interruption rule In addition to controlling non-verbal signals, make it mandatory not to interrupt each other, not even in the heat of the moment. Doing so will help reduce destructive quick reactions that otherwise cut off someone's word and undermine perceived respect for every opinion.
Invite differing perspectives You invite every team member to present hypotheses on why things should—or should not—change. Allow everyone to voice their hypotheses and ideas and discuss them as if you were an objective scientist.
Identify negative bias toward team members and take corrective action Ask yourself: In what ways might I be biased against one or more team members? For example: Who do I consider to know the most about ideal strategies for the firm's future? Who do I allow to voice their opinion, and who might I be implying doesn't have much to contribute? Encourage others to engage in the same reflection and actively counteract biases.
Include breaks when things get tense When social friction increases, team members become exhausted, and discussions stall, call for a break. Allow everyone to return refreshed before you continue the discussion.
Protect the team from groupthink Deliberately assign someone on the team the role of "devil's advocate" to prevent groupthink when discussing the envisioned transformation. Systematically rotate that role among team members.

22 Hadley et al. (2023).

5

Table 5.2 Behavior-oriented action plan to foster psychological safety

	What do we do well? (KEEP DOING)	*What is hindering our effectiveness?* (STOP DOING)	*What should we start doing, or do more of?* (START DOING)
Stage 1: Inclusion safety Concrete behaviors: - … - …			
Stage 2: Learner safety Concrete behaviors: - … - …			
Stage 3: Contributor safety Concrete behaviors: - … - …			
Stage 4: Challenger safety Concrete behaviors: - … - …			

Finally, decide on a **time frame** for testing new behaviors. Throughout the testing phase, observe what works, what people find challenging, and what you need to adjust. Make sure you have **frequent conversations** about how things develop for everyone on the team. These discussions don't need to take up much time. What you want to achieve, however, is this: Psychological safety has to be top of mind for everyone, every day.

Reflect and Act

Consider a team you lead that is currently navigating a significant shift or transformation:

- Which stages of psychological safety do you want to improve for your team?
- What specific behaviors can help achieve this?
- How can you facilitate a conversation with your team about this?

Transform: Foster Psychological Safety Across Your Entire Firm

» Building and reinforcing the work environment where people can learn, innovate, and grow is a never-ending job, but a deeply meaningful one.[23]

By now, you have facilitated a conversation with your team about the results of the psychological safety survey, the areas for improvement, and how to achieve improvements by following an action plan over the next few months. At this point, many leaders believe that, since everything has been put on the table and everyone knows what is expected, levels of psychological safety will automatically rise.

But the hard work is only just beginning: fostering psychological safety requires ongoing effort. Additionally, you now need to implement your action plan with a focus on aligning internal systems and processes—for instance, the performance management system—to eliminate factors that hinder psychological safety.

Never Let Up: Drive Psychological Safety with Persistence

Psychological safety doesn't come naturally; it doesn't just happen. It requires consistent focus and regular reinforcement to remain a priority for everyone. Building a more psychologically safe environment is an ongoing task. It's like in a marriage: Saying *"I love you"* on your wedding day isn't enough—you can't just say, *"See above, I already said it then*", and assume this is enough.

Other industries—where safety in a literal sense is the linchpin—have shown how important it is to continuously work on maintaining and strengthening psychological safety. After several fatal accidents in the **airline industry** in the 1970s, analyses of the flight recorders revealed that someone—often the Captain—hadn't listened to other crew members (co-pilots, or flight attendants) raising a vital safety issue before or during the flight. Or someone had voiced their opinion too late or not at all when the plane was already in free fall. In the 1980s, a training program called **Crew Resource Management** was developed. Its goal was to enhance psychological safety in the cockpit and for every flight attendant. The training focused on improving communication and decision-making, with a strong emphasis on reducing pilot-centered decision-making. It strongly encourages junior crew members to speak up about safety concerns. This training is now mandatory for commercial airlines.

? What lessons can you draw from this for your firm's transformation efforts?

You will have to consistently emphasize why it is crucial for your firm's success that everyone contributes their thoughts, ideas, questions, and critical feedback. It will take time before you can harvest the fruits of your effort. As Amy C. Edmondson

23 Edmondson (2018) (Kindle version) [location 449].

stresses: "*It takes many iterations and forms of communication before employees start to internalize this new way of thinking.*"[24]

Everyone on your team should be exceptionally observant of what is happening: what new behaviors are working, which ones need refinement, and how to respond when team members repeatedly fail to follow the agreed-upon approach.

After the testing period of a few months, you may want to retake the team survey to track progress, discuss what has changed already, and identify where to focus next to further improve psychological safety in your team.

Shape a Psychologically Safe Culture: Align Systems to Enhance Transformative Capacity

For an effective strategic shift from "clients first" to "people first", it is essential to have psychological safety across every level of the firm—the individual level, the level of teams, and the level of the entire organization. You want to have high psychological safety in terms of inclusion, learner, contributor, and challenger safety across the entire organization. Thus, you want to make it an integral component of your firm's organizational culture.

? How do you create a psychologically safe culture?

Since ▶ **Chap.** 3 provides an in-depth discussion on how to transform organizational culture, the following is a brief selection of key aspects to keep in mind when you aim to strengthen a psychologically safe culture:

- Ensure that all formal and informal reward systems are aligned with your emphasis on psychological safety.
- Ensure that any policies implemented in relation to fostering psychological safety will be enforced consistently.
- Communicate consistently about the firm's commitment to psychological safety at all leadership levels (individual, team, firm-wide).
- Focus not only on discouraging behaviors that undermine psychological safety but also on recognizing those that strengthen it—such as acknowledging and celebrating colleagues' efforts, contributions, and achievements to help them feel their efforts are appreciated.
- Solicit and consider feedback from all employees and leaders regularly in a structured way.
- Provide training and development opportunities for everyone in the firm, from practices such as active listening to deeper reflection opportunities for team leaders on how they can model psychological safety and embody the necessary mindsets.

24 Mortensen et al. (2023).

If you succeed in **aligning all systems to foster psychological safety**, it will significantly enhance your firm's transformative capacity. This alignment ensures the firm is much better prepared to effectively manage major changes, whether driven by external factors or arising from an internal need for transformation.

Reflect and Act

- On a scale from 1 to 5, how would you rank the overall level of psychological safety across your entire firm?

1	2	3	4	5
I have to say it is absent in our firm.	*Relatively low levels of psychological safety in most teams in the firm.*	*It is a mixed picture; you can be lucky or unlucky, depending on what team you find yourself in.*	*High level of psychological safety across most of the teams and the leadership of the firm.*	*Very high level across all teams and the leadership of the firm.*

- Are there firm-wide channels and forums where employees can openly share their thoughts and ideas, such as town hall meetings, suggestion boxes, or internal communication platforms? Is feedback from these channels actively encouraged and acted upon?
- When significant failures occur, how does your firm respond? Is there acknowledgment and a constructive analysis to learn from the incident, or is there a tendency to assign blame and move on without deeper analysis?
- Do leaders regularly communicate the rationale behind major decisions and changes within the firm?
- Are members of the firm kept informed and involved in the decision-making process?
- What is one immediate action you can take to further improve psychological safety?

Summary

» A leader's most important job—above that of creating a vision and setting strategy—is to act in the role of social architect and nourish a context in which people are given the respect and permission to feel included, (2) learn, (3) contribute, and (4) innovate.[25]

25 Clark (2020) (Kindle version), p. 39 [location 467].

By leveraging the ACT process, you have now gained a deep understanding of psychological safety, its role in successful transformation, the different levels of psychological safety, and how to improve it within your team and across various levels of your firm.

ACKNOWLEDGE To assess the current level of psychological safety in your team, you

- identified four stages of psychological safety crucial for optimal performance in relation to the planned transformation.
- conducted a team survey to analyze the level of psychological safety across the four stages of inclusion, learner, contributor, and challenger safety.

CHALLENGE To challenge the current status quo of psychological safety in your team, you

- discussed with your team the far-reaching impact of psychological safety on the current transformation effort and specific behaviors that help strengthen psychological safety.
- created an action plan to foster psychological safety in your team with detailed, agreed-upon behaviors to improve psychological safety over the next few months.

TRANSFORM To transform the level of psychological safety consistently across the whole firm, you

- ensured every team member was attentive to the new behaviors, and conducted another survey after a predefined testing period to identify any necessary adaptations for further benefiting from the positive impact of psychological safety.
- created a culture of psychological safety across the entire firm.

References

Clark, T. R. (2020). *The 4 stages of psychological safety: Defining the path to inclusion and innovation.* (Kindle version). Berrett-Koehler Publishers.

Coyle, D. (2018). *The culture code: The secrets of highly successful groups*. Random House LLC US.

Duhigg, C. (2016, February 25). What Google learned from its quest to build the perfect team. *The New York Times*. https://www.nytimes.com/2016/02/28/magazine/what-google-learned-from-its-quest-to-build-the-perfect-team.html

Edmondson, A. C. (1999). Psychological safety and learning behavior in work teams. *Administrative Science Quarterly, 44*(2), 350–383. https://doi.org/10.2307/2666999

Edmondson, A. C. (2018). *The fearless organization: Creating psychological safety in the workplace for learning, innovation, and growth*. (Kindle version) [location 778]. Wiley.

Edmondson, A. C. (2023). *Right kind of wrong: The science of failing well*. (Kindle version). Simon & Schuster.

Hadley, C. N., Mortensen, M., & Edmondson, A. C. (2023, April 25). Make it safe for employees to speak up — Especially in risky times. *Harvard Business Review*.

Herway, J. (2017, December 7). How to create a culture of psychological safety. *GALLUP*. https://www.gallup.com/workplace/236198/create-culture-psychological-Safety.aspx
LeaderFactor. (n.d.). Psychological safety survey. *LeaderFactor*. Retrieved February, 10, 2025, from https://www.leaderfactor.com/psychological-safety-survey
McKinsey & Company. (2023, July 17). What is psychological safety? *McKinsey Explainers*. https://www.mckinsey.com/featured-insights/mckinsey-explainers/what-is-psychological-safety
Mortensen, M., Guadalupe, M., Furr, N., & Bresman, H. (2023, October 09). Effective strategies for building and boosting psychological safety. *INSEAD Knowledge*. https://knowledge.insead.edu/leadership-organisations/effective-strategies-building-and-boosting-psychological-safety
The Fearless Organization Scan. (n.d.). Test the psychological safety in your team. *The Fearless Organization Scan*. Retrieved February 11, 2025, from https://fearlessorganizationscan.com/engage/test-the-psychological-safety-in-your-team
Wang, Y., Liu, J., & Zhu, Y. (2018). Humble leadership, psychological safety, knowledge sharing, and follower creativity: A cross-level investigation. *Frontiers in Psychology, 9*, Article 1727. https://doi.org/10.3389/fpsyg.2018.01727

Guiding Transformative Learning to Enable Growth for People and Teams

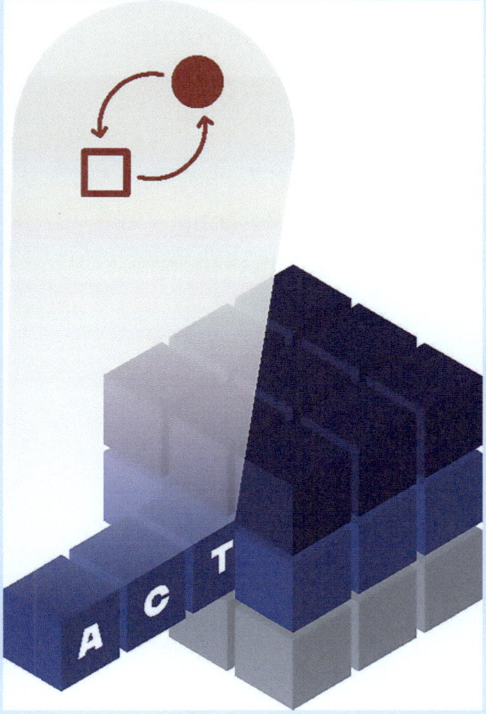

M. Bernhardt, *Leading Transformation in Law Firms*, Law for Professionals,
https://doi.org/10.1007/978-3-031-98653-6_6

Contents

» The illiterate of the 21st century will not be those who cannot read and write, but those who cannot learn, unlearn, and relearn.[1]—Alvin Toffler

? How much of their potential do people actually bring to the workplace?

Research suggests that, on average, **people use only 40% of their performance potential**.[2]

Is 40% enough when leading a transformation that requires significant changes in how people think, act, and collaborate? When the stakes are so high, can individuals and teams afford to leave 60% of their potential untapped?

As a leader navigating transformation, you have the opportunity to change this: to help unlock greater potential and drive meaningful change.

How? The answer lies in helping people and teams embrace transformative learning, empowering them to reach their full potential, seize opportunities, and tackle challenges head-on.

The Power of Deep Learning: Your Competitive Advantage in Transformation

» Learning faster than the pace of change has quickly become an essential skill for surviving and thriving in this ever-changing landscape.[3]

As rapid and constant change has become the norm, it is more important than ever to help individuals and teams learn and develop at their optimal level. As American futurist Alvin Toffler emphasizes, those who thrive in these volatile times are those who can learn, unlearn, and relearn, and who have mastered the skill of adaptability.

Most transformations challenge deeply held assumptions, ingrained work behaviors, and existing paradigms. To thrive, you and your team must embrace the discomfort of questioning what you believe to be true and find the courage to reimagine how things are done. You have to be ready to pull the rug out from under your own feet.

This is where "**transformative learning**"—or "**deep learning**"—comes into play: a meta-skill that enables deep, meaningful shifts in thinking and behavior.

Unlike **simple learning**, which builds incrementally on existing knowledge, transformative learning goes further. By critically examining and reframing taken-for-granted beliefs, assumptions, and behaviors, you unlock deeper levels of engagement, creativity, and problem-solving—indispensable qualities during transformation.

---

1 Goodreads (n.d.).
2 Whitmore (2004), p. 16.
3 Peterson (2022).

Leveraging the ACT Process to Advance Transformative Learning

In the first step (ACKNOWLEDGE), you assess whether a challenge related to a transformation—one that demands changes in behavior and thinking—calls for simple or transformative learning. Then, you help others move into the learning zone, the optimal zone for development and growth.

In the second step (CHALLENGE), you evaluate the current level of learning. Adopting a coaching leadership style, you help individuals and teams gain insights, commit to actions, and enhance their performance.

In the final step (TRANSFORM), you ensure people stay on track with their commitments and foster their ability to use coaching techniques independently. You encourage them to support their team's learning process and contribute to building a firm-wide learning culture.

Acknowledge People's Developmental Needs and Learning Opportunities

Determine Learning Needs and Opportunities that Arise from a Transformation Challenge

Consider the following **scenario**:

You are a Managing Partner and have agreed with one of your fellow partners and practice group leaders, David, that he will lead his practice group's effort to systematically integrate generative AI into their work. Until now, both his core team and the broader practice group have had an excellent reputation. However, they seem to be struggling to incorporate generative AI effectively, leveraging its potential to offer tech-enhanced services and stay competitive.

You realize that David is having difficulty to keep his commitment. He isn't driving new thinking or exploration within his core team or the broader practice group. Progress toward the defined goals to enhance services—increasing internal efficiency, and generating new revenue streams—seems a long way off. Meanwhile, competitors aren't standing still.

These are your observations and interpretations:

- **David seems to want to learn about the potential impact of generative AI, yet he lacks initiative in learning about it**: David signs up for every possible AI training course but always cancels at the last minute. Then, he delegates AI-related questions and tasks to team members, avoiding deeper involvement himself.
- **David oscillates between embracing and ignoring AI-related client expectations**: When clients ask how generative AI could benefit them, David is quick to highlight the practice group's innovation-driven approach and list their accomplishments. But when pressed further, he downplays clients' inquiries, insisting that generative AI, for the most part, isn't yet good enough—reinforcing the value of the current way of delivering services. In your view, this is a misjudgment on

David's part, as he fails to see that client expectations are shifting significantly toward greater efficiency and innovation.
- **David oscillates between encouraging and discouraging generative AI experimentation among team members**: While highlighting the importance of exploring options to integrate generative AI into their work, as soon as problems arise, David shifts course: He discourages his team from continuing their exploration, stops allocating time or resources to generative AI initiatives, and ignores team members' requests to continue exploring the field.

You wonder how best to support David, knowing that—sooner rather than later—his practice group will lose out on the competition if they don't systematically integrate generative AI into their value creation process.

First, you have to be clear about **the characteristics of the challenge** David is facing:
- What skills, mindsets, and behaviors does David need to guide his practice group through the required transformation toward a holistic integration and implementation of generative AI across the value creation chain?
- Does this challenge require David to fundamentally change how he thinks about and approaches this transformation, or will it be enough for him to gain more knowledge about generative AI to better steer the process—without shifting his current perspective on generative AI and its implications for his practice group?

? Will simple learning be sufficient for this kind of challenge or will mastering this challenge require transformative learning?

Option A: **Simple learning will suffice**. Based on what you have observed so far, you may conclude that David lacks information, knowledge, or communication skills needed to successfully support his core team and the entire practice group in systematically integrating generative AI into their work. In an ideal world, you would openly discuss this gap with David, and together, you would agree on a plan to bridge it. Equipped with the necessary knowledge, David would soon be able to drive the transformation across his practice group with the required zest.

Option B: **Transformative learning is required**. Based on what you have observed so far, David is reluctant to move toward a structured integration of generative AI for his practice group, not simply because he lacks knowledge or information. His hesitation seems to be rooted at a much deeper level, as reflected in David's behaviors described above. It appears that David will continue to struggle to empower his team to fully capitalize on the benefits of generative AI unless he significantly shifts his perspective—and with it, his leadership approach to the required transformation.

In Our Scenario it is quite clear that option A won't suffice. David will have to engage in transformative learning to effectively lead the practice group toward new and different ways of generating value by wisely leveraging generative AI.

Reflect and Act

- Based on your experience, which learning challenges are the most difficult to address?
- When was the last time you noticed someone attempting to tackle a challenge through simple learning when it actually required transformative learning?
- How do you typically approach raising someone's awareness of their learning needs, whether for simple or transformative learning?

Operate from the Learning Zone When It Matters Most

Broadly speaking, people tend to be in one of three **mental states—or zones—** when faced with the challenge of changing their behavior and thinking in order to lead and navigate a necessary transformation effectively.

Figure 6.1 presents the Learning Zone Model, which outlines the three mental states: the comfort zone, the learning (or stretch) zone, and the panic (or overstretch) zone.

Comfort Zone

In the comfort zone, you feel safe, know what to do and how to do it.

This is where you can recharge your mental and emotional batteries because you understand how things work. You can effortlessly remain in this zone for long periods.

Fig. 6.1 The Learning Zone Model [Adapted from Vygotsky's (1978) original concept of the 'Zone of Proximal Development']

However, transformation typically pushes you out of your comfort zone. It challenges the way you have done things until now—as well as how you have viewed, interpreted, and made sense of the world. Thus, you won't achieve transformation if you primarily operate from the comfort zone.

At the same time, during a transformation, people often seek opportunities to retreat to their comfort zones because it can be exhausting to feel constantly challenged to adapt, to think, and behave differently.

- **Learning Zone**

However, to effectively learn, you must often move into the **learning zone—or stretch zone**.

In this zone, you will feel more uncomfortable and experience uncertainty or even temporary overwhelm. The greater the perceived uncertainty and complexity, the more you may crave the certainty of the comfort zone. However, it is essential to embrace the discomfort of the learning zone regularly. As Ginni Rometty, former Chairman and CEO of IBM, once said: "*Growth and comfort never coexist. You have to be comfortable with being uncomfortable.*"

- **Panic Zone**

Would it then be optimal to stay in the learning zone continuously? No. If you are constantly stretched and relentlessly pressured to change and learn, you may find yourself in the **panic zone—or overstretch zone**.

In this state, learning becomes difficult because you experience intense emotions that are designed to trigger basic reactions like flight, fight, or freeze. This leaves little room for optimal use of cognitive resources. The best ideas rarely emerge from the panic zone.

Throughout a transformation, people will inevitably find themselves in the panic zone from time to time. As a leader, it is crucial to guide them back into the learning zone, where constructive behavior and effective learning become possible.

To Lead Transformation Effectively you must be skilled at identifying the zones people find themselves in when facing a particular challenge. This will enable you to help them move into the learning zone, without slipping into the panic zone, when necessary.

In Our Scenario to determine how best to support David, you first need to assess whether he is ready to learn at a deep level. This depends on whether he is already in the "learning zone". The zone David finds himself in at the moment will determine how you approach the conversation with him. At present, you suspect that David often operates from the panic zone. David seems to be "all over the place"—wanting to drive the necessary shift in the practice group but then pulling back, oscillating between "pro" and "contra" decisions. You assume he fears making wrong decisions or worries that allowing his practice group to make costly mistakes could damage their excellent reputation in the market.

Your first goal is to help David move from the panic zone to the learning zone, where effective transformative learning becomes possible. For David to engage in transformative learning, he needs to believe that he can successfully lead the practice group through this risky yet potentially highly rewarding transformation.

You begin by having a conversation with David about how both of you perceive the current situation. Together, you explore the thoughts, emotions, experiences, and concerns that bring him into the panic zone—and keep him there. You pay particular attention to helping David recognize the resources he already possesses, reminding him of his past successes in similarly challenging circumstances. You guide him to shift his perspective toward the skills he developed in the past that can now help him learn new skills and mindsets for the current transformation.

This reflection is key for David to become ready to explore how he can more effectively lead the transformation that both his core team and the entire practice group must master.

Reflect and Act

When thinking about a specific transformation you are currently leading:

- When was the last time you found yourself in the panic zone?
- Reflecting on how your team is handling this transformation: What zone(s) do individual team members typically operate from?
- How can you help team members step into the learning zone without slipping into the panic zone, so they can navigate a developmental challenge skillfully?

Challenge the Current Depth of Learning

To help David lead his practice group's shift toward more thoroughly embracing generative AI, you need to challenge the depth of David's current learning.

A key precondition for this conversation is that David trusts you enough to discuss his current struggles openly. Without this foundation, you might not be the right person to support him.

Assuming you and David do have this level of **mutual trust**, agree to keep your conversation **confidential** to ensure both of you can speak candidly.

Coaching Leadership Style: Unlocking Performance Potential

> We live in a world of flux. Successful executives … need to reinvent themselves as coaches whose job it is to draw energy, creativity, and learning out of the people with whom they work.[4]

4 Ibarra and Scoular (2019).

A highly effective tool to support David is adopting the **coaching leadership style,** also referred to as the **"leader-as-coach" approach**. This method is powerful because it helps the other person become aware of and ready to question their own taken-for-granted assumptions. They begin to recognize their default thinking patterns and learn to reframe the challenge they face. By adopting a different perspective, they can decide how to lead the transformation more effectively to achieve its goals.

Coaching is *"unlocking people's potential to maximize their own performance. It is helping them to learn rather than teaching them."*[5]

When you apply a coaching leadership style, you aim for high performance by developing people's abilities to fully draw on their strengths and potential to develop, grow, and act accordingly, focusing on *"future possibilities, not past mistakes."*[6]

Benjamin Zander, a renowned conductor and music coach, beautifully captures a leader's mindset of believing in people's potential to perform:

He gives each of his students a straight *'A'* on the first day of class.

At that point, of course, Zander hasn't heard them play a single note on their instrument.

He describes the 'A' as *"a possibility to live into."*

He believes that every student possesses a tremendous potential that they can unlock, and his role is to assist them in doing so. As Zander puts it: *"I only speak to the 'A' in people and I set as the goal the maximum capacity that people have. I settle for no less. I make myself a relentless architect of the possibilities of human beings."*[7]

However, coaching isn't primarily about *you* believing in the potential of the other person. It is about helping the other person believe in it, too.

One of the strongest internal barriers preventing people from realizing their full potential is a lack of confidence, self-doubt, or fear of failure. Therefore, in every coaching interaction, your aim should be to build the other person's belief in their own potential by embracing **two key principles** of coaching:

- raising the person's **awareness** of the situation: how they interpret it, how they make sense of it, and how they could see it differently.
- raising the person's sense of **responsibility** for addressing the challenge: without fully owning our responsibility, our performance won't improve.

Your key tools as a coach include **listening deeply**—to what is said and to what is left unsaid—paying attention to how it is said, noticing the emotional nuances revealed through voice, language, and non-verbal behavior. Additionally, an effective leader-as-coach *"asks questions instead of providing answers, supports employees instead of judging them, and facilitates their development instead of dictating*

5 Whitmore (2004), p. 8.
6 Whitmore (2004), p. 7.
7 Williams (2014).

what has to be done."[8] You ask **open-ended, potentially transformative questions** to help your colleague gain insights—not from you as the coach, but from within themselves.

This approach is particularly powerful in transformations because it helps unlock a person's performance potential. Especially during transformation, people need to operate at their best to meet demanding goals.

Reflect and Act

- When leading transformation, how much do you focus on people's and teams' potential to perform?
- How often do you use a leader-as-coach approach? With whom? How?
- Who would benefit most from you leveraging the leader-as-coach approach?

The Overconfidence Trap: Why Leaders Overrate Their Skills—And How to Improve

As a leader in the legal profession, you are highly skilled in asking questions. So, shouldn't a coaching leadership style then come naturally to you? Shouldn't you be able to leverage it when needed during a transformation easily?

In one study, 3761 executives were asked to assess their own coaching skills.[9] Their self-assessments were then compared with evaluations from their colleagues and employees.

The results? **24%** of executives *"significantly overestimated their abilities, rating themselves as above average while their colleagues ranked them in the bottom third of the group."*

These executives understood in theory what the coach approach required: "ask and listen", not "tell and sell". However, after years of practicing a more directive leadership style, they defaulted to telling, sometimes in quite creative ways. For example, they often disguised suggestions as leading questions, such as *"Don't you think you could try doing X or Z?"*

The truth is, working with curious, non-leading questions while in a leadership role can be extremely challenging. It is worth remembering that the leaders who most effectively apply the leader-as-coach approach typically acquire the necessary skills and mindset over a more extended period, through dedicated programs and continuous practice.

8 Ibarra and Scoular (2019).
9 Ibarra and Scoular (2019).

Leader-as-Coach in Action: Asking Questions to GROW

In Our Scenario you have supported David in moving into the learning zone, and he is now ready to work on boosting his leadership performance to lead the required transformation within his practice group.

You offer to help David through the leader-as-coach approach, using the **GROW model**—a framework[10] that facilitates transformative learning. This model helps you guide others to perform optimally during challenging times, such as when they need to transform their current ways of creating value for their clients. The process often involves a deep, structural shift in how individuals think, feel, and act.

The acronym **GROW** stands for Goal, Reality, Options, and Will.

Here is how the four sequences of the process unfold:[11]

▪ GOAL Setting: What Is Your Goal?

In the first phase, you help the other person **articulate the aspirations and describe the challenges** they currently experience. You support them in defining specific, measurable, and actionable goals to successfully address the transformation challenge. Together, you agree on these goals.

Without clarity on the goals, neither you nor the other person will know how to measure progress or success.

In Our Scenario as the Managing Partner leading the coaching conversation, you are in a unique role here because you are not an independent coach but, as the name suggests, both a leader and a coach, even if not in the traditional formal supervisory position. In this role, it is entirely legitimate for you to bring in the firm's key objectives. It is also appropriate for you to clearly lay out your expectations.

At the same time, David must have enough space to articulate his own goals, and you both need to honestly assess whether you share the same understanding of the objective.

To maintain a clear focus for the conversation, you have to align on a common goal.

Let's assume that you and David are on the same page and that he genuinely wants to lead his practice group toward a more holistic integration of generative AI into their core processes, even though he is currently struggling.

Learnings at the end of this phase might be:

- David has recognized the importance of having a well-defined goal. He has clarified what he wants to achieve by integrating generative AI in his practice group.

---

10 Whitmore (2004).

11 In practice, you often move back and forth between these four phases. For example, while working on *"options"*, you might realize that the goal is less clear than you initially thought. When this happens, you may need to revisit the *"Goal"* phase to refine it.

- He understands that the goal should reflect both client demands and internal efficiency improvements. His goals are specific, measurable, and aligned with client expectations and the firm's overall strategy.
- David has formulated a clear vision for integrating generative AI in his practice group in a way that aligns with the firm's broader strategic objectives.

REALITY: What Is the Current Reality?

This phase involves a thorough **examination of the current situation and its broader context**. By asking curious questions, you encourage the other person to reflect on how they perceive the situation, and what assumptions they are making about it. Together, you uncover what has helped them in the past to successfully handle similar challenges, and what resources they possess to tackle the current challenge (e.g., knowledge, skills, people, networks, finances).

Learnings at the end of this phase could be:

- David has clearly analyzed the inconsistency in encouraging AI experimentation within his team while failing to provide sustained support.
- He has identified his behavioral pattern of oscillating between embracing and dismissing the idea of fostering generative AI integration—between wanting to learn more and hesitating to fully commit to the learning process.
- He has acknowledged the internal barriers to achieving his goals, such as concerns about making mistakes during AI implementation and potentially damaging the practice group's reputation.
- David understands that his fear of being unable to keep up with the pace of technological advancements—and the possibility of making himself redundant—is further contributing to his reluctance.
- He has begun to shift the assumptions that led to his oscillating behavior and is now embracing a perspective focused on actively influencing the transformation process. He draws on his past experiences, as well as the resources within his team and the practice group, to achieve the transformation goal.

OPTIONS: What Options Do You Have?

In the third phase, you help the other person **explore strategies to achieve their transformation goal**. You encourage them to brainstorm various approaches to overcome obstacles. This phase fosters your colleague's creativity and divergent thinking.

Exploring different options allows your colleague to consider new perspectives and opens them up to opportunities they may not have seen before.

During this phase, asking, *"What else could you do?"* repeatedly can be highly effective in stimulating exploration. Research shows that you can use this question more often than you might think, as it usually prompts new ideas even when the person's initial response is, *"I don't know."*

Learnings at the end of this phase might be:

- David has identified various strategies to overcome the challenges he described in the previous phase. By considering these options, he has explored actions he hadn't previously thought of that could help bridge the gap between the current situation and his goal.

- Some of the options David is now considering include: partnering with teams and practice groups across the firm that have more experience with generative AI to learn from them; establishing clear project goals with timelines to maintain momentum and focus within his team; assigning someone on his team the explicit role of monitoring David's behavior and immediately reminding him when he exhibits unhelpful tendencies that discourage his team from continuing their exploration; setting up a client feedback loop to gain insights into their expectations and experiences; and setting aside dedicated time each week to deepen his knowledge of generative AI and its implementation.

WILL: What Will You Do?

In the final phase, you help the other person narrow down their options and translate new insights and perspectives into tangible behaviors and practices. They **commit to specific actions** and agree on exact timelines for carrying them out. This phase also involves setting up mechanisms for accountability and support.

Learnings at the end of this phase could be:

- David has discussed with you how to ensure his intentions translate into consistent action and corresponding performance for both himself and his practice group.
- David has decided on those options he wants to concentrate on and has committed to taking concrete steps to advance them.
- He has laid out an action plan with a clear timeline. For example, he will lead weekly check-ins with his practice group to discuss current issues, challenges, progress, and next steps. He will also align the group's efforts with client expectations by setting up a client feedback loop to ensure their initiatives meet evolving client needs.

Reflect and Act

- Have you worked with the GROW model or a similar framework before?
- What questions have you found particularly powerful?
- When using the GROW model, which of the four phases do leaders in your firm most often tend to skip when supporting others in mastering transformation?

Guided by you through the GROW process, David gains clarity on his goals, acknowledges his current blockers, explores viable solutions, and commits to specific actions that will lead to the successful integration of generative AI into his practice group.

Feelings Are Facts: Navigate Emotions Without Judgment

While leading David through the GROW process, you will want to pay close attention to the emotional side of learning.

Emotions are data, just like any other form of information. When you approach emotions the same way you approach any other important data, the coaching process will have a much greater positive impact.

> If we have learned anything about learning, we've learned that it's not an isolated, rational process that is cold, dry, and mechanistic. Emotion is nested in reason, and reason in emotion. Cognition and affect are inseparably connected.[12]

When leading a coaching conversation, emotion-related challenges are twofold: **First, you have to manage your own emotional tensions.** As a leader in an exposed position, you may catch yourself having thoughts such as:

- I want to look smart by asking the best questions that stimulate completely new thinking for David.
- I should recommend a course of action to David.
- It feels uncomfortable that I don't know exactly how the integration of generative AI into David's practice group's work could be implemented.

Feelings of insecurity, concern, or frustration might accompany these thoughts. Strong and stressful emotions can negatively impact your ability to stay open, curious, and non-judgmental.

Emotion regulation and impulse control will be your key tools to overcome the urge to "fix the problem" by quickly suggesting a solution that may not actually work for David.

To achieve this, resist the impulse to immediately analyze and judge. Quick judgments often arise from an evaluating thought paired with an emotional reaction.

Curiosity is the natural antidote to these self-centered impulses. Instead of focusing on your thoughts and emotions, redirect your attention to David's perspective. Curiously listen to him, seek to understand his train of thought, and explore options that may help him achieve his goal.

Withhold the urge to be helpful by providing answers. In the leader-as-coach role, your strength lies not in delivering solutions or smart answers, but in fostering a joint, curious exploration of what might be possible for David.

Second, you support the other person to manage their emotional tensions. David may also struggle with thoughts such as:

- I should know exactly how to proceed.
- I want to look smart by providing the best answers that showcase my deep expertise to my colleague. I fear appearing less confident and knowledgeable than I would like.

12 Clark (2020) (Kindle version), p. 81 [location 1032].

- I am concerned that the practice group's fantastic reputation—which we worked so hard to build—will suffer irreparably if we make mistakes or wrong decisions while exploring value-creation opportunities. And I am unsure how to manage this risk.

Accompanying emotions might be self-doubt, embarrassment, anxiety, or helplessness.

As a leader who adopts a coaching role, your job is to not dismiss any of David's thoughts or emotions as irrational, unfounded, or *"wrong"*. Instead, you create a safe space for David to voice these concerns. Only then will he be able to examine the assumptions underlying his concerns. Only then will he be able to adjust these assumptions, enabling a more courageous exploration of the benefits that generative AI could bring to the practice group, clients, and the firm.

Transform Learning Sustainably

By leading David through the GROW process, you have helped him shift some of the fundamental assumptions that were holding him, his team, and the entire practice group back from making substantial progress toward the defined transformation goal.

Keep the Momentum: Encourage Ongoing Improvement

With David's decisions in phase four of the GROW model, both of you might be tempted to believe that things will now develop as planned. However, David is likely to experience ups and downs. He may find it more difficult to stick to his commitments than expected.

In your role as leader-as-coach, you agree on **regular and frequent touchpoints** with David to maintain momentum. Whenever David encounters hurdles, you will be ready to engage in another—likely much shorter—coaching conversation to help him stay on course. You continue to leverage your leader-as-coach skills by providing David with space to reflect on setbacks and explore ways to overcome them.

Your approach will likely lead to a **trickle-down effect** in two ways:

David's capacity for self-coaching: By using the leader-as-coach approach, you aim to enhance David's ability to navigate and master typical challenges and setbacks throughout a transformation. Having experienced the value of the coaching format, David will begin to use more of the tools himself. He will ask himself more open-ended questions, reflect on assumptions that may hinder his progress, and develop workable action plans without needing your direct support.

David's impact on his team and the practice group: Before long, David will start applying this approach with team members who are struggling to adapt to the transformation. He will leverage his coaching skills to ignite transformative learning within his team and across the practice group, ensuring they develop and perform optimally throughout the transformation.

In this way, you have contributed to a culture of learning that extends beyond David.

Build a Culture of Constant Learning and Growth

The ability to coach individuals and teams is essential to creating a learning organization where learning is embedded in all organizational structures and processes.

> To transform your company into a genuine learning organization, you need to do more than teach individual leaders and managers how to coach better. You also need to **make coaching an organizational capacity** that fits integrally within your company culture. And to succeed at that, you must effect a cultural transformation.[13]

In 2019, Herminia Ibarra, professor at London Business School, described a shift toward a learning culture at the law firm Allen & Overy [now A&O Shearman], *"where year-end appraisals and rankings had become a largely unproductive ritual…, the firm … abandoned that performance review system and now trains its partners to engage year-round in coaching conversations with associates… Employees report that these conversations create a new and useful level of dialogue about their career development."*[14]

The specific structure of coaching conversations has also proven helpful in other contexts, as Ibarra explains: *"Although the program was designed for internal use, it has made the organization's senior leaders more comfortable in conducting unstructured conversations in other contexts, especially during high-stakes client negotiations—and that, in turn, has led to higher revenue and deeper client relationships."*[15]

You and your fellow leaders shape your firm's organizational culture.

ⓘ If your culture strongly emphasizes transformative learning and adaptability in the face of significant change and transformation, your firm will possess the most significant competitive advantage imaginable in today's world.

Summary

You have now gained a deep understanding of the impact of transformative learning on high performance during transformation challenges. You strengthened others' deep learning to help them elevate their performance sustainably.

13 Ibarra and Scoular (2019) [emphasis added].
14 Ibarra and Scoular (2019).
15 Ibarra and Scoular (2019).

ACKNOWLEDGE To recognize the nature of the challenge and the required way of learning, you

- determined the characteristics of the challenge and the learning needs of the other person.
- assessed the *"zone"* the other person was operating from and supported their shift toward the learning zone to prepare them for effective transformative learning.

CHALLENGE To question and elevate the current level of learning, you

- leveraged a coaching leadership style to guide the other person through a transformative learning experience using the *"GROW"* framework.
- supported the other person in creating a concrete and measurable action plan to achieve their transformation goal.

TRANSFORM To sustain transformative learning across individuals, teams, and the firm, you

- secured the other person's ongoing commitment to the transformation goal by providing regular opportunities to discuss and adjust their action plan as needed.
- helped them apply the coaching leadership style not only to themselves but also to their team.
- contributed to cultivating a culture of transformative learning across the entire firm, helping raise performance levels sustainably.

Fostering transformative learning will enhance your firm's ability to respond effectively to the heightened dynamics of significant change and transformation—whether it involves adapting to and creating new business models, forging innovative ways to create value, implementing new technologies, designing radically different multidisciplinary workflows, or navigating various forms of Human-AI collaboration.

By strengthening the learning capabilities of individuals, teams, and the firm as a whole, ultimately, you position your organization to navigate the complexities of transformation, overcome obstacles, and achieve its objectives.[16]

---

16 The concept behind this idea is commonly referred to as *"Organizational resilience"*. For more information, please refer to Barasa et al. (2018).

References

Barasa, E., Mbau, R., & Gilson, L. (2018). What is resilience and how can it be nurtured? A systematic review of empirical literature on organizational resilience. *International Journal of Health Policy and Management, 7*(6), 491–503. https://doi.org/10.15171/ijhpm.2018.06

Clark, T. R. (2020). *The 4 stages of psychological safety: Defining the path to inclusion and innovation*. (Kindle version). Berrett-Koehler Publishers.

Goodreads. (n.d.). *Quote by Alvin Toffler*. Retrieved February 12, 2025, from https://www.goodreads.com/quotes/8800-the-illiterate-of-the-21st-century-will-not-be-those

Ibarra, H., & Scoular, A. (2019). The leader as coach. How to unleash innovation, energy, and commitment. *Harvard Business Review, 97*(6), 110–119.

Peterson, D. B. (2022). Future-proof yourself for complex, disruptive times: Learning faster than the pace of change. In B. Underhill, J. Passmore, & M. Goldsmith (Eds.), *Coach me! Your personal board of directors: Leadership advice from the world's greatest coaches*. Wiley. https://doi.org/10.1002/9781119823803.ch49

Vygotsky, L. S. (1978). Original concept of the 'Zone of Proximal Development', as presented in *Mind in Society: The Development of Higher Psychological Processes*. Harvard University Press.

Whitmore, J. (2004). *Coaching for performance: Growing human potential and purpose*. Nicholas Brealey Publishing.

Williams, D. (2014). *50 stories & snippets for conference & workshop presentations*. (Kindle version). Self-published.

Building Teams that Drive Transformation with Collaboration and Emotional Foresight

M. Bernhardt, *Leading Transformation in Law Firms*, Law for Professionals,
https://doi.org/10.1007/978-3-031-98653-6_7

Contents

» Great things in business are never done by one person. They're done by a team of people.[1]—Steve Jobs

The innovation team was thrilled to introduce their latest service to their biggest client: a cutting-edge AI tool designed to draft contracts in seconds.

At first, the client seemed intrigued. *"This would be fantastic"*, he admitted. But as he listened to the details, his excitement faded. *"Wait—our systems aren't compatible with your platform. We can't even use it."*

Key Challenges Impacting Team Performance During Transformation

? How do these numbers resonate with you?

Around **80%** of employees' workdays are spent in **teams**.[2] **86%** of executives claim that **ineffective collaboration and communication** are the major causes of failure in business.[3] **75%** of cross-functional teams are **dysfunctional**.[4]

Steve Jobs' Insight remains highly relevant—in fact, this has never been more true: in modern law firms, lasting success rarely results from individual brilliance, but cohesive, high-performing teams. And in today's dynamic business environment, effectively leading cross-functional teams has become even more crucial. A recent white paper by Simon-Kucher & Partners, in collaboration with the Bucerius Center on the Legal Profession, explores how generative AI will disrupt traditional business models of law firms.[5] The authors claim that law firms will need to resemble corporations more in the future, with "*greater division of labor, more centralized steering and authority, and more sophisticated go-to-market and monetization models.*"[6]

In this context, they emphasize the importance of leaders skillfully leading cross-functional teams:

» Leadership skills are becoming increasingly important in managing cross-functional teams. All interviewed Managing Partners agreed that effective leadership of such teams is essential.[7]

1 CBS News (2003).
2 Cross et al. (2016).
3 Salesforce Canada (2014).
4 Tabrizi (2015).
5 Simon-Kucher & Partners in collaboration with Bucerius Center on the Legal Profession (2025).
6 Simon-Kucher & Partners in collaboration with Bucerius Center on the Legal Profession (2025), p. 14.
7 Simon-Kucher & Partners in collaboration with Bucerius Center on the Legal Profession (2025), p. 17.

A key resource in transformations is effective, high-performing teams that tackle external challenges impacting your firm and drive internal transformation initiatives, such as:

- shifting the firm's focus toward providing more personalized and client-centric services
- implementing generative AI across the firm's technological infrastructure and processes
- creating a more inclusive and diverse work environment
- expanding the firm's market presence through a merger
- shaping a more collaborative firm culture.

What Are Key Components of High-Performing Teams?

A high-performing team involves a small number of people with complementary skills who are committed to a common purpose, a set of performance goals, and an approach for which they hold themselves mutually accountable.[8] To achieve their common purpose, the team has to effectively collaborate and communicate. It has to be able to raise morale and alignment in challenging times, engage skillfully with all key stakeholders, and provide constant development and learning opportunities for its members and the team as a collective.[9]

Given the rising relevance of collaboration in multi-disciplinary and cross-functional teams for successful transformation, a key question arises:

? How do you effectively ignite team performance, allowing teams to be prepared for and thrive in transformation?

Three Major Challenges Can Significantly Hinder Transformation Success

Let's look at each in turn:

Challenge No. 1: Narrow Internal Team Focus

Often, team leaders focus on the internal functioning of a team—defining clear goals and roles, establishing processes, accountability, fostering supportive relationships, and ensuring sufficient diversity in team composition. Most executive team leadership trainings highlight these criteria, often assuming that once these elements are in place, the rest will follow.

8 Katzenbach and Smith (2015).
9 Hawkins (2017).

However, problems arise when leaders focus too narrowly on creating strong team cohesion:

A team may develop an overly internal focus, concentrating on internal team dynamics while neglecting what happens beyond their confined space. They fail to see what other teams in the firm are working on or how that might relate to their work. They don't seek out that information. They overlook whether their transformation project aligns with the firm's broader strategy. They disregard diverse perspectives and dismiss those who challenge their approach. In doing so, they become an **encapsulated nucleus**—driving a transformation that is largely disconnected from the rest of the firm.

This is when, *"Building internal cohesion in the team becomes a liability when the team ignores developments in the outside world."*[10]

At worst, this could mean designing a client solution that proves unusable because it is disconnected from the client's real needs.

By contrast, when a team balances strong internal cohesion with a strong external focus, it is constantly aware of and responsive to everything happening:

(a) Inside of the firm:

- What are other teams in the firm currently working on?
- How does the firm's strategy impact our transformation project?
- What does the firm's leadership want and need from us?
- How do different stakeholders in the firm need to be involved?
- Who do we need to convince of our goals?
- Who is giving us valuable critical feedback?

(b) Outside of the firm:

- What do key stakeholders think about the envisioned transformation?
- What can they contribute, and what can we learn from them?
- Which experts could we consult?
- What is the competition doing—both within and beyond our industry?
- How is the ecosystem evolving, and what are the potential implications for the transformation process and its success?

Research highlights that *"**when adapting to rapidly shifting external conditions** or implementing a new strategy, **an exclusively internal focus can be lethal**. When success depends on keeping up with technology, markets, competitors, and other external stakeholders, an external focus combined with an internal focus is essential."*[11]

A strong **integration of external and internal focus** is a characteristic of teams that are extremely successful in driving innovation[12] for their firms.

For example, studies across various industries showed that when team member interactions were tracked via wearable devices, teams that were more able to build

10 Ancona and Bresman (2023) (Kindle version).
11 Ancona and Bresman (2023) (Kindle version), p. 24 [location 424] [emphasis added].
12 Ancona and Bresman (2023).

and sustain networks across and outside the firm achieved greater productivity and higher levels of innovation.[13]

So, as a leader, you want to skillfully orchestrate for your team to consistently adopt a strong integrated—internal and external—focus to best steer the transformation.

▪ Challenge No. 2: Unsupportive Team Environment

Naturally, team leaders tend to focus on who is part of the team and how the team works together. However, creating an environment that supports optimal team performance is equally critical. This includes:

- **aligning internal organizational systems** that measure and reward performance with the expectations set for teams. For example, does the reward system focus solely on individual achievements, or are there tangible rewards for effective teamwork?
- **shaping a strong organizational culture** that reinforces the behaviors teams need to be successful. For instance, does the firm's cultural environment encourage low-threshold interactions between teams or practice groups? Does it highlight the importance of continuous learning and development?

Additionally, the level of **psychological safety** is a key environmental factor in team performance (see also ► **Chap.** 5 on how to foster psychological safety). The more you foster **trust** among team members, the more likely they are to ask tough questions when it matters, challenge existing ways of interacting, and provide honest critical feedback. Thus, psychological safety directly influences team communication.

It also impacts whether team members are willing to assume leadership responsibilities based on their expertise, regardless of formal titles. A flexible approach, known as **distributed leadership**, ensures that leadership responsibilities are assigned to those best suited for the respective task—empowering individuals to take on leadership roles during each phase of a transformation. Distributed leadership has proven highly effective in transformations, because where *"keeping your finger on the pulse of technology and changing markets is critical, … leadership needs to be spread across many players, both within and across organizations, up and down the hierarchy—wherever information, expertise, vision, commitment, and new ways of working together reside."*[14]

As a senior leader, your role is to lead by example and support other team leaders in creating a supportive environment. After all, without the right environment, no team can effectively navigate the challenges of transformation.

---

13 Pentland (2012).

14 Ancona and Bresman (2023) (Kindle version), p. 4 [location 191].

- **Challenge No. 3: Neglect of Emotional Success Factors**

Recent research by EY and Oxford Saïd Business School has shown that **organizational transformation is, largely, an emotional journey** affecting everyone's behavior.[15] Emotions can range from fascination to frustration, excitement to exhaustion, and from experiencing feelings of "resistance" to feeling energized by the idea of being part of a transformation. Without exception, every team member, stakeholder, and client experiences emotions in relation to a transformation.

To successfully steer a transformation, it is essential to leverage emotions as you would any other data.

? How can you support teams to skillfully handle emotions during a transformation?

To perform at their best, teams have to develop **Team Emotional Intelligence** (TEI), defined as the *"ability of a group to develop a set of norms that manage emotional processes"*.[16] Team Emotional Intelligence extends beyond individual emotional intelligence: it encompasses the emotions within the team, as well as those of stakeholders inside and outside the firm.

As a team leader, you can actively promote norms that help your team effectively handle emotions, emphasizing how a group's emotional awareness and regulation drive higher team effectiveness and performance.[17]

Leveraging the ACT Process to Create High-Performing Teams

When leading a team that is driving transformation, your job is to tackle the three challenges described.

As a senior leader, you are wearing several hats. At times, you will lead a team yourself and/or collaborate with other team leaders in the firm. Sometimes, you will apply the ACT process to your own team; at other times, you will support other team leaders in recognizing and addressing specific team challenges in transformations.

In the first step of the process (ACKNOWLEDGE), you assess your team's current focus. Is it primarily centered on internal dynamics, or is it equally focused on stakeholders inside and outside the firm? Additionally, you observe how effectively the current team environment supports team interaction, emotional management, and distributed leadership.

In the second step of the process (CHALLENGE), you scrutinize what changes your team needs to make for optimal performance in relation to the three challenges.

Finally, in the third step of the process (TRANSFORM), you decide on concrete action steps to help team members adapt behaviors that will sustainably enhance team performance.

15 White et al. (2022).
16 Druskat and Wolff (2001a), p. 133.
17 Druskat and Wolff (2001b), p. 82.

Acknowledge Current Team Focus and Blind Spots

In the first step of the process, you assess the status quo of your team's focus and gain a deeper understanding of the blind spots that may hinder optimal team performance.

Gain a 360° Perspective: Assess Team Focus from Every Angle

To analyze where your team currently stands, you adopt a 360° view that encompasses four angles—outward, inward, around, and inside. You reflect on questions pertaining to all four angles to ensure you get as holistic a picture as possible.

Start by reflecting on the following questions yourself. Then, invite each team member to go through them individually. This will help you gain insight into each person's perspective and allow the team to develop a deeper awareness of how members perceive current teamwork.

▪ Look Outward

When looking outward, you focus on the **external environment**—all factors outside your team. You observe and assess how your team interacts with other teams in your firm, internal and external stakeholders, and the broader ecosystem. You also consider the competitive landscape and how the team gathers information outside the firm.

This focus relates to the challenge no. 1, described above.

These questions can help you more fully understand how your team currently operates in relation to its external environment:

- To what extent does this team collaborate with other teams, practice groups, or sector groups across the firm?
- How do they gather information from these other teams, practice groups, or sector groups?
- How does the team gather information from outside the firm?
- How do they ensure continuous exploration and inquiry, rather than closing off information gathering too soon?
- What external environmental factors (e.g., regulations) does the team need to take into account?
- Who will be affected by the process and/or outcome of the transformation, both inside and outside the firm?
- Who are the key players in the ecosystem the team needs to consider?
- What does the competitive landscape look like for the team?

▪ Look Inward

Now, you assess the **dynamics and interactions within your team**, including how skillfully emotions are managed.

This focus relates to the challenges no. 2 and no. 3, described above.

The following questions can help you gain a deeper understanding of your team's internal dynamics:

(a) **Norms around communication & interaction**

- Does your team have explicit norms for communication?
- How do team members currently communicate within the team?
- Which channels do they use, and how often?
- Does the team primarily focus on formal, task-oriented communication, or does it also allow for informal conversations?
- Does your team have clear norms around team emotional intelligence—addressing individual team member's emotions, the team's collective emotions, and key stakeholders' emotions? Do these norms help the team understand, manage, and leverage emotions effectively?

(b) **Team Composition**

- Is it clear who is part of the team—and who isn't?
- How interdisciplinary, cross-functional, international, or otherwise diverse is the team?
- What are the implications of the team composition for the envisioned transformation?
- What specific strengths does the team have, and what challenges does it face?
- In what ways might the team composition need to change in the course of the transformation?

(c) **Clarity of goals, roles, and responsibilities**

- Does your team have clear goals for the envisioned transformation?
- Are team members aware of their specific roles and responsibilities?
- How committed are they to achieving the goal?

(d) **Processes, Structures, and Routines**

- What patterns of collaboration have emerged in this team over time?
- What processes, routines, or structures has the team established?
- Which of these will support the team during the transformation, and which might hinder performance?

Look Around

What is the **impact of the immediate team environment**? Do internal processes, structures, and reward systems help the team coordinate and execute effectively? Does the level of psychological safety empower team members to challenge each other's perspectives—honestly voicing concerns and criticism? Does the environment enable team members to assume distributed leadership flexibly?

This focus relates to challenge no. 2, described above.

These questions may guide your reflection:

- What behaviors do firm-wide systems reward, and which do they discourage?
- How does the reward system influence interactions within your team, behavior toward other teams, and interactions with external stakeholders?
- In what ways does the firm's culture support collaborative teamwork, both inside and outside the firm?
- To what extent is psychological safety established in this team? Are people allowed and empowered to contribute ideas, questions, and concerns without fear of disapproval?
- Are team members encouraged to assume distributed leadership, regardless of formal titles?
- What similar transformations have team members experienced within the firm in the past?
- What lessons from these experiences might apply to the current transformation?

▪ Look Inside

Based on your experiences and observations of the team, you assess your perceptions of both **individual team members and the team as a whole**. When looking inside, you examine your own assumptions, emotions, and motivations regarding the team, all of which inevitably affect and shape your interactions.

Each team member should also engage in this kind of **honest reflection** to better understand how they relate to individual team members and the entire team.

This focus relates to all three challenges described above.

The following questions can support this reflection:

- What are my thoughts, ideas, and emotions toward this specific team? For instance, do I see it as a "dream team", or have I become discouraged by previous disappointments?
- What motivates me to work with this team?
- What concerns do I have regarding my role and performance within the team?
- What drains my energy when working with this team, and why?
- What do I think—and how do I feel—about the envisioned transformation?
- Considering the envisioned transformation, do I experience or anticipate "resistance" from others, whether team members, internal stakeholders, or external stakeholders?
- What might I be avoiding to see when reflecting on how the team will achieve the envisioned transformation?

Reflect and Act

Thinking of a team you are currently working with to drive transformation in your firm:

- Which of the four angles is your team focusing on right now?
- Which angle might the team currently be neglecting?

	1	2	3	4	5
360° view of team collaboration	*Not at all*	*Much to improve*	*So-so*	*Quite good*	*Five-star rating*
Look outward— To what extent does your team have an integrated—internal and external—focus?					
Look inward— To what extent has your team established explicit norms for interaction?					
Look around— To what extent does the immediate environment support collaboration within the team and across the firm?					
Look inside— To what extent are individual team members aware of their motivations and beliefs that influence performance?					

- Which angle could your team focus on even more to collaborate successfully and achieve the envisioned goal?
- What is one action you can take right now to help your team improve in that area?

Challenge Team Behaviors and Define Key Action Steps

Having assessed the four angles, you and your team dive deeper into current behavioral habits that might hinder effectiveness, and explore how to use the team's resources to improve performance. Together, you identify key areas the team needs to address to achieve the transformation goal and decide how to get started.

Look Outward: Question the Current Scope of Focus

If your assessment has revealed that the team is operating with too narrow a focus, consider discussing the questions in ◘ Table 7.1 to detect the specific factors currently hindering top performance.

After this discussion, decide which current team behaviors enhance performance and benefit the envisioned transformation (**keep doing**), which behaviors should be discontinued (**stop doing**), and which new behaviors the team should adopt or strengthen (**start doing**) to advance team performance.

Look Inward: Scrutinize the Current Level of Team Emotional Intelligence

Teams face various challenges when dealing with emotions during a transformation. They must attend to **emotions on three levels**:
- individual team members
- the team as a whole
- other teams and key stakeholder groups, inside and outside the firm.

A team's emotional intelligence extends beyond the sum of each individual member's emotional intelligence.

ⓘ When teams effectively leverage emotional intelligence across all three levels, they significantly improve performance and strengthen collaboration, commitment, and creativity.[18]

Teams with higher levels of team emotional intelligence communicate more effectively, make better decisions, and handle conflict without compromising team goals.[19] Moreover, they are more accepting of divergent viewpoints,[20] better at motivating each other, and more adept at building rapport with others.[21]

? How often does your team experience **positive emotions**?

Positive emotions—such as joy, inspiration, gratitude, interest, pride, and compassion—are powerful motivation and performance boosters. Specifically, emotions:
- build cognitive resources, which enhance concentration, creativity, and focus.[22]
- broaden people's modes of thinking.[23]
- improve cooperation, increase group effort, and reduce conflict.[24]

---

18 Druskat and Wolff (2001a), p. 133; Druskat and Wolff (2001b), p. 82.
19 Barczak et al. (2010) and Rego et al. (2007).
20 Suliman and Al-Shaikh (2007).
21 Dulewicz and Higgs (2000).
22 Fredrickson (2013).
23 Fredrickson (1998).
24 Barsade (2002).

Table 7.1 From current to desired team focus: key behaviors

	What do we do well? (KEEP DOING)	What is hindering our effectiveness? (STOP DOING)	What should we start/do more of? (START DOING)
How do we currently …			
analyze developments, changes, threats, and opportunities in the ecosystem?			
gather information within the firm, including key stakeholders' expectations?			
gather information outside the firm, including external key stakeholders' expectations?			
leverage internal feedback—both the feedback we provide and the feedback we receive?			
leverage external feedback—both the feedback we provide and the feedback we receive?			
manage information flow across the firm and all hierarchy levels?			
keep key internal stakeholders informed about progress and challenges?			
keep key external stakeholders informed about progress and challenges?			
coordinate tasks across lateral connections, functions, and interdependent units within and outside the firm?			
communicate the benefits and challenges of the transformation?			
ask for help (e.g., financial, human resources, mentoring) and leverage internal support for the transformation?			
ask for help (e.g., financial, human resources, mentoring) and leverage external support for the transformation?			
celebrate, appreciate, and reward team members and the whole team for their contributions?			

- enable effective collective coping with stress[25]—when we feel emotionally supported, we can surpass our own limits when facing a challenge.
- advance constructive social interactions[26] and strengthen relationships, leading to higher commitment and engagement.

To examine the current level of emotionally intelligent team behaviors, discuss the team's level of emotional awareness, regulation, and the prevalence of positive emotions, as outlined in Table 7.2.

Ensure you create a space where team members feel comfortable sharing emotions. Practice deep listening, ask open-ended questions, and paraphrase what you have understood. This approach helps regulate everyone's emotions during the discussion.

Table 7.2 Assessing team emotional intelligence through observable behaviors

	What do we do well? (KEEP DOING)	What is hindering our effectiveness? (STOP DOING)	What should we start/do more of? (START DOING)
Emotion awareness			
How aware are we of each individual's emotions? How does that show?			
How aware are we of the team's overall emotional state? How does it show?			
How aware are we of cross-boundary emotions from external teams and stakeholder groups we interact with? How does it show?			
Emotion regulation			
How well do individual team members regulate their emotions? How does it show?			
How effectively does the team as a whole regulate emotions? How does it show?			

(continued)

25 Lansisalmi et al. (2000).
26 Cunningham (1988).

Table 7.2 (continued)

	What do we do well? (KEEP DOING)	What is hindering our effectiveness? (STOP DOING)	What should we start/do more of? (START DOING)
How well does the team support external teams in effectively regulating their emotions? How does it show?			
Promoting positive emotions			
How strongly do we each focus on experiencing a sufficient number of positive emotions—such as joy, pride, contentment, and excitement— throughout the day? How does it show?			
How well do we, individually and as a team, support other team members in experiencing a sufficient number of positive emotions throughout the day? How does it show?			
How well do we, as a team, support external teams in experiencing a sufficient number of positive emotions throughout the day? How does it show?			

Look Around: Investigate the Environment's Impact on Team Performance

Psychological safety is a key environmental factor that impacts communication, learning, and conflict resolution within the team (see also ▶ **Chap.** 5 on how to foster psychological safety).

Many of the questions in Table 7.3 directly address this critical component.

After discussing these questions, determine which team behaviors enhance performance and support the envisioned transformation (**keep doing**), which behaviors the team should no longer continue (**stop doing**), and which new behaviors the team should adopt or strengthen (**start doing**) to advance team performance.

Table 7.3 Assessing the environment's impact on team behaviors and performance

	What do we do well? (KEEP DOING)	What is hindering our effectiveness? (STOP DOING)	What should we start/do more of? (START DOING)
How do we demonstrate that we value each team member, regardless of their background, experience, or other attributes?			
How do we encourage open communication and participation from everyone, including quieter members?			
How do we respond when people ask questions, seek clarification, or admit mistakes?			
How do we facilitate feedback and learning?			
How do we support team members so they feel empowered to contribute ideas without fear of being dismissed?			
How do we ensure all team members have equal access to resources and opportunities they need to contribute effectively?			
How do we handle conflicts or disagreements within the team?			
How do we respond to individuals who challenge established ways of doing things?			

Additionally, recognize your pivotal role in shaping psychological safety within your team. Reflect on what actions you can take to further strengthen this essential foundation for high team performance.

Look Inside: Determine Each Member's Behavioral Impact on Team's Effectiveness

With a substantial level of trust within the team, you can take this a step further by asking individual team members to reflect on the discussion so far and **commit to**:

- one specific behavior they will adopt moving forward—a behavior that will help the team make progress on a critical aspect discussed.
- one behavior they will stop displaying in the future—a behavior that is hindering team effectiveness.
- one behavior they will continue practicing—a behavior that contributes positively to team performance.

With high trust across the team, making these commitments public can be powerful.

Moreover, team members can hold one another accountable, provide encouragement, and offer support when someone struggles to shift certain behaviors.

Reflect and Act

Which of the four perspectives—outward, inward, around, or inside—do you find most challenging in a team you are currently working with on a transformation?

- Start a conversation with your team about how they perceive their interactions in this regard.
- Ask each team member to identify one behavior they will commit to in order to help the team enhance its capabilities and achieve the transformation goal.

Transform: Sustainably Shift Team Behavior

Your team has now committed to working on the areas identified as critical to high performance. To help your team adjust behaviors and sustain these changes, it is essential to agree on concrete actions.

You can **use the four angles**—outward, inward, around, and inside—**to take a 360° view** and steer the conversation within your team.

When addressing the question of team focus, you may want to discuss the questions in ◘ Table 7.4.

Look Outward: Embrace a 360° View and Transform Team Behaviors

Specify the exact goals, tasks, resources, and risks to ensure every team member is aware of their individual and collective responsibilities, activities, and challenges to monitor.

Table 7.4 Creating an action plan: aligning internal, external, and integrated team focus [The structure of the table—goals, tasks, resources, and risks—is based on the "Team Alignment Map", a very powerful tool introduced by Mastrogiacomo and Osterwalder (2021)]

360° view	Goals (What)	Tasks (Who)	Resources (How)	Risks to avoid
How will we ensure we have a rigorous process for analyzing developments, changes, threats, and opportunities in the ecosystem?				
How will we ensure we fully understand expectations from key stakeholders inside and outside the firm?				
How will we ensure we continuously manage the flow of information upward, downward, laterally, and outward?				
How will we ensure we ask senior leaders and other stakeholders inside and outside the firm for regular feedback?				
How will we ensure we coordinate tasks appropriately across all lateral connections, functions, and interdependencies with other units within and outside the firm?				
How will we ensure we know when to ask for help (e.g., financial, human resources, mentoring) and leverage support for the transformation—internally and externally?				

7

Look Inward: Establish Norms to Strengthen Emotional Flexibility

To further enhance your team's emotional intelligence, consider establishing norms that create a foundation for effective and seamless collaboration—as Druskat and Wolff (2001b) put it, *"helping otherwise skilled teams fulfill their highest potential."*[27]

Discuss with your team which norms they find appropriate and agree that team members will mutually uphold these norms and remind each other when they are violated.

Table 7.5 outlines two types of norms:

- norms that create awareness of emotions
- norms that help regulate emotions.

27 Druskat and Wolff (2001b), p. 79.

Table 7.5 Establishing norms that strengthen team emotional intelligence [Adapted from Druskat and Wolff (2001b)]

Level	Norms that create awareness of emotions	Norms that help regulate emotions
INDIVIDUAL Individual team members	**Foster interpersonal understanding**, for instance through: – regular check-ins at the beginning of meetings where you explicitly invite people to share how they are doing – asking for clarification of emotions when members use abstract terms like *"annoyed"* to better understand whether they are, for example, frustrated, exhausted or sad.	**Be ready to confront team members** who disrespect agreed-upon rules by: – gently but firmly addressing misbehavior – encouraging all team members to be both compassionate and clear, not judging others but constructively addressing behavior – modeling the behaviors you want to see in others.
TEAM Your team as a whole	**Gather feedback** from inside or outside the firm and discuss it openly, using insights to identify and address emotional barriers that may hinder the team's progress.	**Create space for conversations about emotions** by discussing difficult emotions as they arise, using techniques such as deep listening and reframing to help team members regulate their feelings.
CROSS-BOUNDARY External teams your team interacts with	**Increase organizational understanding** by reflecting on how culture impacts the team's emotional effectiveness, discussing which emotional responses are *"typical"* of the culture and how they influence collaboration.	**Foster opportunities for interaction with other teams** by actively asking what they need from your team, offering and providing support whenever possible.

Both operate on all three levels of team emotional intelligence:
- individual team members' emotions
- the team's collective emotions
- the emotions of other teams and key stakeholder groups inside and outside the firm.

Look Around: Help Your Team Engage in Distributed Leadership

As a team leader, you will want to ensure that the most qualified team members take the lead on specific tasks at different phases of the transformation. To foster team members' readiness to assume distributed leadership, consider the following actions:

1. ensure a shared understanding of the transformation goals among all team members. If the goals are unclear, it is much more difficult for team members to recognize when a shift in leadership is necessary.
2. align team objectives, contributions, dependencies, and potential risks, for example, using a Team Alignment Map[28] that covers goals, tasks, resources and risks to avoid (as outlined in ◘ Table 7.4).
3. provide regular feedback and coaching. To support team members who assume leadership roles, leverage the "leader-as-coach" approach as discussed in ▶ **Chap.** 6. Coaching helps team members grow into leadership roles.
4. recognize and reward distributed leadership. Celebrate instances where team members take initiative and successfully lead in their areas. This reinforces desirable leadership behaviors.
5. emphasize the importance of reflection to further improve team performance: The better team members understand how they and others think, feel, and act, the better they relate to one another within and outside their team. They will also become more adept at building and sustaining relationships with those they temporarily lead and by whom they are led at other times.
6. encourage leadership development, both formal and informal: To help team members gain more confidence in their leadership capabilities, encourage them to closely observe those who excel at distributed leadership. Enable their participation in executive development programs whenever possible to deepen their understanding of leadership roles and responsibilities.
7. foster an environment of psychological safety: Without psychological safety, team members may hesitate to assume leadership roles because these roles expose them more than simply being a team member. Cultivate an environment where team members feel safe to step up, take risks, and lead without fear of failure or judgment.

Look Inside: Encourage Team Members to Improve Internal Awareness

To further support team members in enhancing their awareness of thoughts and emotions, regulating their emotions effectively, and reframing their thinking to improve collaboration, you can leverage your skills as "leader-as-coach" (see ▶ **Chap.** 6). With curious and open questions, help team members detect detrimental behavioral tendencies that might otherwise go unnoticed.

In addition, strengthening your own internal awareness allows you to credibly model the behaviors you wish to see in others. To achieve this, you can also draw on various techniques discussed in ▶ **Chap.** 8 in relation to the development of a growth mindset. Moreover, by observing the impact your behavior has on your team, you can also assess whether you are—perhaps unintentionally—displaying

28 Mastrogiacomo and Osterwalder (2021).

leadership behaviors that limit your team's performance potential (see ▶ **Chap.** 9 on unintentionally diminishing leadership behaviors).

Track Efforts to Adapt Team Behaviors During the Transformation

The more precisely you measure progress related to the team's commitments, the easier and faster it will be to adapt when necessary.

Ensure you track the team's progress in collaboration and performance, linking their efforts to tangible business outcomes.

To do this, use an action plan to clearly define the outcomes you and your team aim to achieve by adapting specific team behaviors.

Summary

You have now gained a deep understanding of three key challenges that often arise when a team leads a transformation—challenges that can negatively impact a team's effectiveness and performance.

You have leveraged the ACT process to assess your team's current level of functioning across four perspectives—outward, inward, around, and inside—identified the areas your team needs to improve and supported them in transforming their current interactions to enhance their positive impact and achieve their transformation goal.

ACKNOWLEDGE To assess the team's current functioning, you

- evaluated their focus across four perspectives—outward, inward, around, and inside.
- invited team members to reflect on how they perceive team performance in relation to the four perspectives.

CHALLENGE To scrutinize specific team behaviors that may hinder performance, you

- discussed with your team its current level of performance in relation to the four perspectives, and identified what they should keep, stop, and start doing to improve team performance.
- decided with the team which behaviors need to change to help them perform better collectively.

TRANSFORM To sustainably shift team behaviors, you

- agreed on an action plan including concrete steps for each of the four perspectives to ensure every team member knows how to contribute to the team's effectiveness.

- supported team members with various leadership tools, such as the "leader-as-coach" approach, to enhance their performance.
- committed to consistently monitoring progress to sustain improvements.

Creating sustainable high-performing teams may well be one of the most daunting tasks for leaders. Systemic influences—within team members, within the team, across and outside the firm—add immense complexity.

Therefore, closely observing team dynamics, continuously reflecting on and adapting your leadership behavior, and engaging in an open discussion with your team will be tremendously valuable to improving team performance and engagement.

References

Ancona, D., & Bresman, H. (2023). *X-Teams: How to build teams that lead, innovate, and succeed.* (Kindle version). Harvard Business Review Press.

Barczak, G., Lassk, F., & Mulki, J. (2010). Antecedents of team creativity: An examination of team emotional intelligence, team trust and collaborative culture. *Creativity and Innovation Management, 19*(4), 332–345. https://doi.org/10.1111/j.1467-8691.2010.00574.x

Barsade, S. G. (2002). The ripple effect: Emotional contagion and its influence on group behavior. *Administrative Science Quarterly, 47*(4), 644–675. https://doi.org/10.2307/3094912

CBS News. (2003). *Steve Jobs in his own words. 60 Minutes.* https://www.cbsnews.com/news/steve-jobs-in-his-own-words/

Cross, R., Rebele, R., & Grant, A. (2016). Collaborative overload. *Harvard Business Review, 94*(1–2), 74–79.

Cunningham, M. R. (1988). Does happiness mean friendliness? Induced mood and heterosexual self-disclosure. *Personality and Social Psychology Bulletin, 14*, 283–297. https://doi.org/10.1177/0146167288142007

Druskat, V. U., & Wolff, S. B. (2001a). Group emotional intelligence and its influence on group effectiveness. In C. Cherniss & D. Goleman (Eds.), *The emotionally intelligent workplace* (pp. 132–155). Jossey-Bass.

Druskat, V. U., & Wolff, S. B. (2001b). Building the emotional intelligence of groups. *Harvard Business Review, 79*(3), 80–90. https://hbr.org/2001/03/building-the-emotional-intelligence-of-groups

Dulewicz, V., & Higgs, M. (2000). Emotional intelligence: A review and evaluation study. *Journal of Managerial Psychology, 15*(4), 341–372. https://doi.org/10.1108/02683940010330993

Fredrickson, B. L. (1998). What good are positive emotions? *Review of General Psychology, 2*(3), 300–319. https://doi.org/10.1037/1089-2680.2.3.300

Fredrickson, B. L. (2013). Positive emotions broaden and build. *Advances in Experimental Social Psychology, 47*, 1–53. https://doi.org/10.1016/B978-0-12-407236-7.00001-2

Hawkins, P. (2017). *Leadership team coaching: Developing collective transformational leadership.* Kogan Page.

Katzenbach, J. R., & Smith, D. K. (2015). *The wisdom of teams: Creating the high-performance organization*. Harvard Business Review Press.

Lansisalmi, H., Peiro, J. M., & Kivimaki, M. (2000). Collective stress and coping in the context of organizational culture. *European Journal of Work and Organizational Psychology, 9*, 527–559. https://doi.org/10.1080/13594320050203120

Mastrogiacomo, S., & Osterwalder, A. (2021). *High-impact tools for teams: 5 tools to align team members, build trust, and get results fast*. Wiley.

Pentland, A. (2012, April). The new science of building great teams. *Harvard Business Review.* https://hbr.org/2012/04/the-new-science-of-building-great-teams

Rego, A., Sousa, F., Pina e Cunha, M., Correia, A., & Saur-Amaral, I. (2007). Leader self-reported emotional intelligence and perceived employee creativity: An exploratory study. *Creativity and Innovation Management, 16*(3), 250–264. https://doi.org/10.1111/j.1467-8691.2007.00435.x

Salesforce Canada. (2014, August 20). How soft skills are crucial to your business. *Salesforce*. https://www.salesforce.com/ca/blog/how-soft-skills-are-crucial-to-your-business/

Simon-Kucher & Partners in collaboration with Bucerius Center on the Legal Profession. (2025). *The AI-Conomics of legal services. How generative AI will transform the commercial model of law.*

Suliman, A. M., & Al-Shaikh, F. N. (2007). Emotional intelligence at work: Links to conflict and innovation. *Employee Relations, 29*(2), 208–220. https://doi.org/10.1108/01425450710720020

Tabrizi, B. (2015, June 23). 75% of cross-functional teams are dysfunctional. *Harvard Business Review*. https://hbr.org/2015/06/75-of-cross-functional-teams-are-dysfunctional

White, A., Smets, M., & Canwell, A. (2022, July 18). Organizational transformation is an emotional journey. *Harvard Business Review*. https://hbr.org/2022/07/organizational-transformation-is-an-emotional-journey

Individual Level

Contents

Embracing a Growth Mindset to Fuel Opportunity-Driven Transformation

Contents

M. Bernhardt, *Leading Transformation in Law Firms*, Law for Professionals,
https://doi.org/10.1007/978-3-031-98653-6_8

» Progress is impossible without change; and those who cannot change their minds cannot change anything.—George Bernard Shaw

» A man will be imprisoned in a room with a door that's unlocked and opens inwards; as long as it does not occur to him to pull rather than push.[1]—Ludwig Wittgenstein

When was the last time you didn't pull a door knob that would have opened new opportunities for you and your firm during a period of significant change and transformation?

As Wittgenstein insightfully suggests, it's not a lack of ability that holds us back in moments of change—but the mindset we bring to the challenge.

Mindset: A Key Lever for Organizational Transformation

A mindset is *"the mental attitude that shapes our actions and thoughts."*[2] It consists of assumptions and beliefs that reflect how you think about yourself, others, and the world. It is your specific *"frame of mind"*—the lens through which you view the world. A mindset significantly influences what you think, feel, decide, and how you behave in nearly every situation.

As the quote from George Bernard Shaw so sharply reminds us, meaningful transformation begins in the mind. **According to research by EY and Saïd Business School (University of Oxford), a leader's awareness of their assumptions about and attitude toward change[3] is a key lever for successful organizational transformation**. Leaders in this study emphasized the importance of recognizing *"the limitations of your current mindset and capabilities, given the transformational challenge you're facing."*[4]

The pivotal impact of mindset on transformation success becomes evident not only in large-scale organizational transformation but also in smaller initiatives.

Consider the Following Scenario **Emma**, a fellow partner, is determined to transform how her team collaborates and shares leadership responsibilities. Rather than relying on formal roles or titles, she wants leadership to emerge naturally, based on expertise. This approach will allow the team to fully leverage its diverse skills and perspectives, ensuring that the most qualified person takes the lead on any given task. It will also foster a more agile, responsive team—one where leadership is fluid, and responsibility shifts dynamically based on the challenge at hand.

1 Wittgenstein (1980), p. 42.
2 Wolińska-Skuza (2022) (Kindle version), p. 16 [location 118].
3 White et al. (2023) [emphasis added].
4 Saïd Business School and EY (2022), p. 14 [emphasis added].

Emma is convinced that, over time, this kind of flexible leadership will enhance the team's ability to tackle complex projects more effectively.

She actively encourages every team member to step up when their expertise is needed and urges them to seek opportunities to grow their leadership skills.

However, when team members attempt to do so but struggle with their new leadership responsibilities, Emma quickly becomes impatient, lamenting their lack of instant expertise. She is quick to judge: *Obviously, leadership isn't for everyone.*

Deep down, Emma believes people either have the skills to lead, or they don't. More specifically, she assumes that "introverted" individuals are less capable leaders than "extroverted" ones.

This mindset manifests in her behavior: When team members hesitate or struggle while attempting to lead, Emma frequently takes over decision-making herself or delegates tasks to one highly "extroverted" senior associate whom she fully trusts.

Over time, "introverted" team members disengage, and some leave the team altogether.

Emma's fixed mindset undermines her goal to strengthen flexible leadership in her team, ultimately **weakening her team's ability to navigate complex challenges during transformation**. By holding onto her own assumptions about who can lead, she reinforces the very leadership bottleneck she set out to eliminate.

Is Your Mind Set for Transformation?

You have likely come across articles urging leaders to adopt a flexible, adaptive mindset to lead transformation successfully. Sometimes, respective mindsets are referred to as innovation, entrepreneurial, digital, agile, customer-centric, collaborative, risk, inclusive, curiosity, or problem-solving mindset.

At their core, these beliefs stem from **two overarching mindsets**—the growth mindset and the fixed mindset.

Growth Mindset

Carol S. Dweck, professor at Stanford University, coined the term growth mindset. She defines it as the belief that skills, talents, and abilities can be significantly developed through effort, learning, and support from others.[5]

ⓘ The following assumptions reflect a growth mindset:

- I encourage my peers to take calculated risks, knowing that this will lead to valuable lessons, even if the outcomes aren't always successful.

5 Dweck (2017) (Kindle version), p. 16 [location 195].

- I believe every member of my team—including myself—has the potential to develop and excel beyond their current capabilities.
- I encourage my associates to lead meetings and projects, helping them develop leadership skills.

Adopting a growth mindset and fostering it within your firm is a key lever for transformation success, whether at the individual, team, or organizational level.

For example, Satya Nadella, CEO of Microsoft, led its organizational culture transformation with a relentless focus on fostering a growth mindset across the organization.[6]

Fixed Mindset

By contrast, a fixed mindset is the belief that abilities, intelligence, and talents are fixed traits that cannot be developed or changed noticeably over time. Individuals with a fixed mindset often feel compelled to prove their worth repeatedly because, ultimately, *"if you have only a certain amount of intelligence, a certain personality, and a certain moral character—well, then you'd better prove that you have a healthy dose of them."*[7] They evaluate every situation by asking themselves: *"Will I succeed or fail? Will I look smart or dumb? Will I be accepted or rejected?"*[8]

The following assumptions are symbolic of a fixed mindset:

- I doubt that people can change much from who they originally are, even with extensive training.
- I do not encourage associates to take on complex cases as I feel they lack the experience needed to handle them effectively.
- I assume that admitting I don't know something will reduce my credibility among peers and employees.

Most of us hold a mix of both growth and fixed mindsets. You might be absolutely convinced that other people can change but equally convinced that you cannot. Or you might have a growth mindset in certain areas and a fixed mindset in others.

6 O'Reilly (2024).
7 Dweck (2017) (Kindle version), p. 15 [location 187].
8 Dweck (2017) (Kindle version), p. 16 [location 195].

Reflect and Act

- To what extent do you believe intelligence can increase?

Not at all	Rather disagree	It depends	Mostly agree	Fully agree

- To what extent do you evaluate yourself based on learning progress rather than only results?

Not at all	Rather disagree	It depends	Mostly agree	Fully agree

- To what extent do you believe failures can lead to positive outcomes in the long run?

Not at all	Rather disagree	It depends	Mostly agree	Fully agree

- What goals do you want to achieve in developing and transforming your firm?
- Where could shifting your mindset help you better reach those goals?

8

Your Mindset Governs How You Lead Transformation

According to research, **leaders often lean into a fixed mindset in complex, high-stress situations**, becoming more controlling, and less open or curious.[9]

Transformations often qualify as complex, high-stress situations: They disrupt what you believe to be 100% true, how you think about important skills, criteria for success or failure, and the value of learning. Leaders and teams have to learn, unlearn, reskill, and upskill; they have to collaborate, communicate, and work in ways that differ substantially from the past.

Imagine you have a fellow partner, **Sasha,** who **is vocal about the necessity of transforming the firm's current approach toward new technologies**. She believes everyone in the firm should experiment more, take more responsible risks, and learn from failure when working with new technologies.

Yet, whenever it comes to immersing her team in new technologies, she claims, *"Right now, we cannot afford to make mistakes that could impair our performance"*. Deep down, Sasha believes it is inherently dangerous for her team to experiment and test because she doesn't trust them to skillfully handle and correct mistakes and learn from failure. This fixed mindset impacts her behavior as she sends mixed messages to her team, leaving them confused about the appropriate level of experimentation with new technologies. When mistakes occur, Sasha immediately starts pointing fingers. The result is a substandard level of testing new applications, as

9 Miller (2019).

everyone avoids making mistakes instead of focusing on making progress through feedback and adaption.

> You cannot credibly lead transformation unless your mindset and actions are aligned—and unless you visibly model the change you expect from others.

If you lead transformation from the stance of a fixed mindset, you may inadvertently produce the following negative outcomes:

- avoiding transformation initiatives that involve substantial challenges due to their unknown outcome
- failing to encourage people to develop their skills, overlooking the fact that a temporary decline in performance is often a natural part of acquiring the skills that are critical to transformation success
- frequently stepping in to fix problems because you don't believe others can handle them
- being in constant firefighting or micromanaging mode, leaving yourself and others overworked and stressed.

Over time, people and teams lose motivation and commitment to the transformation. Performance declines, ideas stop flowing freely, and innovation stalls. People miss opportunities to expand their potential to reach the next performance level.

Moreover, you may unconsciously foster a culture of fear and mistrust—one where people doubt what you say and fail to buy into the stated transformation goals.

In Contrast **when you lead transformation with a growth mindset**,

- you provide adequate feedback, and support individual and collective development because you believe everyone can learn, change, and grow
- you promote effective communication across the firm, encourage open dialogue and idea exchange, enabling you to quickly adjust the course of a transformation if needed
- you don't look for anyone to blame when something goes wrong
- you systematically strengthen your own ability to change and serve as a role model for others who need to shift their behaviors or mindsets during a transformation.

By consistently behaving this way, you shape a culture of learning and adaptability in your firm which is essential for any successful transformation (see also ▶ Chap. 3 on how to shape a strong and adaptive culture).

Table 8.1 summarizes how a growth versus fixed mindset can impact your leadership during transformation.

Table 8.1 Impact of fixed versus growth mindsets on leadership behavior in transformation

Fixed mindset	Growth mindset
You see **failure** during a transformation **as a sign of incompetence** and lack of intellect. Success in a transformation effort proves you are smart while failure signals incompetence.	You see **failure as a valuable learning opportunity** and a stepping stone towards mastery and transformation success. This is not to say you seek mistakes but recognize they are inevitable for learning.
You **don't deliberately provide learning opportunities** for others during a transformation. When people make mistakes, you are quick to judge them as incompetent, and people start hiding mistakes from you.	You **provide multiple learning opportunities** to support development during a transformation. When others make mistakes, you respond in ways that help them learn from them, feeling safe admitting them.
You reject **criticism** during a transformation or ignore it as you don't believe you can learn from it. You don't actively seek feedback from others.	You **respond well to criticism** and setbacks during a transformation because you frame these experiences as opportunities for growth rather than as threats.
You **don't give feedback** to others, or you do so in a way that doesn't allow them to see how they can improve.	You consistently provide **constructive feedback**, including critical feedback, because you believe people can improve and grow with its help.
You **avoid reasonable risks** that are often inherent in a transformation, such as testing new strategies that might need adjustment on the way.	You are willing to **take calculated risks** when you lead transformation, learn from the outcomes, and tolerate uncertainty during the process.
You **advise others to refrain from taking risks**, even in situations where doing so is essential for innovation to emerge.	You **encourage others to take balanced risks** when this is crucial for learning and adapting quickly to a changing environment.

8

Reflect and Act

- Where do you see fixed-mindset thinking within your firm, and how can you address it as a leader?
- How do you model a growth mindset for your partners and teams in times of uncertainty and transformation?
- What specific leadership challenges have tested your ability to maintain a growth mindset during transformation?
- Which aspects of your leadership style reinforce a growth mindset in your team, and where might you unintentionally reinforce a fixed mindset?

Leveraging the ACT Process to Transform Your Mindset

Mindsets influence how we approach transformation and determine how we handle the inevitable challenges that come with significant change.

In the first step of the ACT process (ACKNOWLEDGET), you recognize mindset limitations in relation to the specific transformation you aim to achieve. You use non-judgmental questions to detect previously unchallenged assumptions, applying focused attention to catch your thinking in real time.

In the second step (CHALLENGE), you question your mindset by adopting the attitude of a scientist who objectively distinguishes facts from beliefs. You use transformative questions to gain new perspectives, explore alternative behavioral options, and shift your mindset.[10]

In the third step of the process (TRANSFORM), you translate your adapted mindset into concrete behaviors. You evaluate the impact of these behaviors and adjust them if needed.

Acknowledge Mindset Limitations to Transformation

? How often do you think about your thinking?

Unless you catch your thinking in real time, it is almost impossible to change it.

Interestingly, most of us are quick to recognize when others need to adapt their thinking:

Let's take another look at **Sasha**, your fellow partner: it might be obvious to you that her team needs to test new technologies, mistakes included.

At the same time, I suspect you recall situations where you caught yourself thinking:

"Learning, failing, mistakes are all important."

Only to add, *"But **this** transformation project isn't the right one for such a learning journey."*

Or *"But this team is **not yet** ready to test new approaches responsibly."*

Or *"But today is not a good day for testing; I might let them work with more autonomy ... **tomorrow**."*

While most of us find it easy to spot when others' mindsets and behaviors hinder progress, we often find it much harder to recognize when our own mindset needs to adapt.

---

10 The literature does not clearly distinguish between *mindset transformation*, *mindset shift*, and *mindset change*. "*Mindset transformation"* suggests a deeper, more comprehensive adaptation of one's mental frameworks, whereas a "*mindset shift"* implies an adjustment in thinking—potentially significant, but not necessarily as profound as a transformation. "*Mindset change"*, by contrast, is a broader term that encompasses any modification in one's mindset, regardless of its impact. From my perspective, the terminology matters less than the actual process: transitioning from a mindset that hinders transformation to one that actively supports meaningful change.

Sharpen Your Focus to Catch Thoughts in Real Time

» Qui-Gon Jinn, a character in Star Wars: Episode I – The Phantom Menace, famously stated, "Your focus determines your reality."[11]

? How quickly do you detect thinking habits that can get in the way of effectively leading transformation?

The sooner you recognize the impact of your mindset on your leadership effectiveness, the sooner you can adjust it if needed.

Reflect and Act

Considering your past weeks at work, on average:

- How deliberately could you focus your attention throughout the day?

1	2	3	4	5
Not at all	I rarely succeed	It depends	Very well	I am a five-star expert in this

- How easily could you switch focus, for example, from thoughts to emotions or sounds in your environment?

1	2	3	4	5
Not at all	I rarely succeed	It depends	Very well	I am a five-star expert in this

- How long did it take you to realize that you intended to focus on one thing but drifted to something entirely different?

1	2	3	4	5
"*Very long*" would be an understatement	Quite long; I typically don't realize it until much later	It depends	I catch it quickly	I realize it immediately

- What is one small change you could make to further improve your focus?

The ability to focus your attention can be developed through consistent **attention focus training**, also referred to as "present moment awareness"[12] or "mindfulness" training.

11 Lucas (1999); for a scientific approach to focus, see Newport (2016).
12 Brassey et al. (2020).

Mindfulness is a metacognitive capacity[13] that allows you to monitor and regulate your thinking and emotional processes. It involves **noticing and accepting your inner experiences** in the moment **without immediately judging** your thoughts, feelings, or other experiences.[14]

Research on mindfulness has grown substantially over the past 30 years. If you regularly train your focus, you can:

- improve attention control and concentration[15]
- strengthen emotion and impulse regulation[16]
- advance rational decision-making[17] and reduce cognitive biases
- enhance creativity[18]
- sharpen problem-solving ability.[19]

Interestingly, even a brief mindfulness practice—20 min daily for 4 days—enhances the ability to sustain attention over longer periods.[20]

It is important to find your own way to train focus. Meditation is but one option. You can train your focus while taking a walk in a forest, climbing a steep face, or engaging in other deliberate activities. Whatever activity you choose, the goal is to direct your attention deliberately in the moment, ultimately enabling conscious leadership when it matters most.

Don't Fight Your Inner Reality: Accept It to Adapt It

Imagine your alarm clock rings at the pre-set time. What happens if you ignore it?

At first, the sound increases slightly. But if you don't respond, it grows steadily louder, demanding your attention until it becomes impossible to ignore. Accepting that your alarm is ringing—instead of burying yourself under the sheets wishing it wasn't—is an appropriate first response.

> Similarly, accepting your thoughts and emotions in relation to a specific transformation is a necessary prerequisite for ultimately deciding to adjust them.

13 Gibbons (2019) (Kindle version), p. 304 [location 3898].
14 Brassey et al. (2020).
15 Lazar et al. (2005) and Ricard et al. (2014).
16 Grecucci et al. (2015).
17 Bechara and Damasio (2005) and Huang (2017).
18 Colzato et al. (2012).
19 Ren et al. (2011).
20 Slagter et al. (2007).

Reflect and Act

Choose one thing you want to focus on, such as surrounding sounds or an image you are looking at:
- Can you maintain focus for 10 s?
- For 30 s?
- For one minute?

Reflect on your experience:
- How easy or difficult was this exercise?
- How quickly did you notice your mind wandering?
- How well were you able to refocus on what you wanted to concentrate on?

Make a commitment to yourself:
- When is the best time of day for you to train your focus?
- For how many seconds or minutes are you willing to practice?
- How will you ensure you follow through on your commitment to sharpen your focus?

Recognize Your Taken-for-Granted Assumptions

At their core, mindsets involve specific assumptions. **An assumption** is a particular type of thought taken as true without proof and, therefore, typically not questioned. Assumptions are often built on prior knowledge, beliefs, or cultural norms and serve as filters. A core assumption influences subsequent thoughts, emotions, decisions, and behaviors related to it.

To fully recognize your mindset, be curious about what you are thinking. **Curiosity**—the strong desire to know about something[21]—**is closely tied to the skill of asking open-ended questions**, such as:
- What am I thinking?
- What am I feeling?
- What assumptions am I making?

Why should you be aware of your emotions when uncovering your mindset? Because **thoughts and emotions are intrinsically connected**. Together, they often reveal the core assumptions underlying your mindset more precisely than focusing on your thoughts alone.

According to research by Saïd Business School (University of Oxford) and EY,[22] to lead transformation effectively, you have to acknowledge your emotions

21 Oxford University Press (n.d.).
22 White et al. (2023).

early on. Otherwise, subconscious emotions can get in your way when you are least prepared for it:

» You need to be brutally honest about the fear, anxiety, and self-doubt you feel about what you can and can't do, what you do and don't know, and therefore what you need to learn. You also need to be aware of your relation to and emotional impact on others. By understanding your own emotional landscape and how to regulate and transform it, the better you will be at having a positive impact on others.[23]

Let's return to the example of your fellow partner **Emma,** who wants her team to grow by embracing flexible leadership. She catches herself thinking about a team member, Thomas, whom she considers to be a "high introvert", the following: *"Thomas will never be able to lead a meeting effectively because he is too introverted."*

She pauses to examine the emotions that accompany this thought and realizes she feels anxiety, doubt, and impatience. Accepting these emotions without trying to suppress or change them, she asks herself: *What do I believe to be true about this situation and about Thomas?*

Emma realizes she holds the assumption that strong leadership requires extroversion and that introverted people can't effectively lead. Deep down, she doesn't fully embrace the idea that leadership skills can be developed or that different personalities can lead successfully.

This insight helps Emma recognize her fixed mindset about leadership and its impact on her team's development and performance.

Reflect and Act

Consider a specific transformation-related situation:

1. Acknowledge your thoughts:
   - What are you thinking about the situation?
   - What are you thinking about yourself?
   - What are you thinking about others?

2. Acknowledge your emotions:
   - What emotions arise for you?
   - What thoughts could help you accept these emotions?

3. Acknowledge your mindset and its assumptions:
   - What assumptions become apparent to you? For example:
     "I believe/am convinced that ________________________________."
     "I am convinced that people want ________________________________."
     "I believe that I have to ________________________________ in order to be successful."

23 Saïd Business School and EY (2022), p. 14.

Challenge Unquestioned Beliefs of Your Mindset

> » If you don't change your mind frequently, you're going to be wrong a lot.[24] – Jeff Bezos

By now, you have uncovered your mindset along with its specific assumptions.

Now is the time to challenge your core assumptions—because, as Jeff Bezos points out, failing to do so undermines the cognitive flexibility needed to adapt to new realities.

A great way to do this is by **identifying and exploring typical mindset traps**.

Using the "scientist mode", you can avoid these traps and instead consider new, previously unnoticed perspectives.

Adopt a Scientist Mode

8

Three particularly powerful mindset traps can limit your success in transformation. They often surface when we present or receive an idea. Psychologist Philip E. Tetlock describes these mindset traps as "preacher" mode, "prosecutor" mode, and "politician" mode.[25] Operating from these modes makes it difficult to listen effectively. Instead, you may impose your ideas on others and react defensively if your idea doesn't receive immediate applause. Quite often, we succumb to these traps subconsciously. Here is an overview of these mindset traps:

- **The Preacher Mode**

When **someone challenges your fundamental beliefs** about yourself, others, or the world, you instinctively defend them. You deliver lengthy arguments about why your views are correct. Listening to others becomes almost impossible when you are in broadcasting mode.

- **The Prosecutor Mode**

When **you spot inconsistencies in someone's reasoning**, you attack their point of view to win the argument. If a peer provides an idea that you believe to be unfounded, you automatically start picking it apart.

- **The Politician Mode**

When **you seek to influence or win over a group**, you passionately advocate for your cause and try to gain their approval. You focus on what you believe is the right decision for the future, but you fail to balance your perspective with differing views.

Countering Mindset Traps with the Scientist Mode Adam Grant, psychologist and professor at the Wharton School, proposes a fourth mode, the **scientist mode**,

24 Bariso (2017).
25 Tetlock (2002).

which enables you to gain new perspectives.[26] In scientist mode, you **broaden and objectify your perspective**, ultimately allowing yourself to adapt your assumptions. You systematically **question your beliefs** and remain open to updating them based on new evidence. This mode of thinking, or mindset, helps you accept that your current assumption might not be the only or the correct one. It also enables you to hold multiple contrasting perspectives simultaneously.

When you operate in scientist mode, **you naturally embody a growth mindset**. You are confident that you can adapt your thoughts and learn to think differently if necessary.

? Why is it called scientist mode?

Scientists, too, value their hypotheses. But in scientist mode, you don't seek to prove the validity of your hypothesis at all costs. You carefully frame your thoughts as hypotheses that you can test and evaluate objectively. With the help of powerful questions, you actively search for new and different perspectives, and even evidence that might disprove your hypothesis.

Researchers at Bocconi University studied the **impact of the scientist mode on performance—including revenue generation**—in Italian startups.[27] They ran an experimental study with over 100 Italian startup founders, all of whom participated in a 4-month entrepreneurial program.

Half of them were trained to adopt a scientist mode, using scientific methods for decision-making, including developing hypotheses, conducting rigorous tests, and using data to predict the success of their ideas.

The other half, the control group, relied on traditional heuristics, intuition, and less structured approaches.

The results showed that entrepreneurs applying a scientist mode performed better, generated more revenue, better mitigated their cognitive biases when analyzing market signals, and strongly improved their decision-making precision.[28]

Reflect and Act

- During a transformation, what are typical situations where you tend to operate in preacher, prosecutor, or politician mode rather than scientist mode?
- When was the last time you applied a scientist mode during a transformation?
- What was the outcome?

Use Transformative Questions to Reframe Your Thoughts

? What makes the scientist mode so powerful?

26 Grant (2021) (Kindle version), p. 19 [location 326].
27 Camuffo et al. (2019).
28 Todesco (2019).

With the help of transformative questions, you can shift the frame of your thoughts, **reframe** them, and adopt a different perspective. Think of reframing as painting over an existing image with new colors and shapes or putting on a pair of glasses to see it with fresh focus. This ability is at the heart of effectively transforming your mindset.

In **high-performance sports**, athletes use reframing to view adversity and setbacks as challenges to overcome, enhancing their frustration tolerance and boosting performance in competition.[29]

The scientist mode enables you to let go of unhelpful mindsets with the help of transformative questions, such as:

- What evidence supports my assumption?
- What evidence speaks against it?
- What evidence am I overlooking?
- What am I afraid to see or admit?
- What do I not know?
- How might I be wrong?
- How might someone else view this specific situation from a different standpoint?

Curiosity, questioning, and openness to new insights are three essential ingredients for developing the ability to reframe a challenge in your transformation efforts and shift your mindset. You are far more likely to come up with questions that help you shift your mindset when you are genuinely curious about the answers. And you are curious only when you are truly open to new insights that may come up during your exploration.

Reflect and Act

To challenge your mindset using the scientist mode, revisit the assumptions you have identified through your reflections so far:

- Distinguish facts from beliefs:
  - What evidence supports your assumption?
  - What evidence speaks against it?
  - What evidence might you be overlooking?
  - Which perspectives are you leaving out?
  - How might you be wrong?
  - What would you think or do if you had no fear of consequences?
  - What else could you think, feel, or do?

- Identify new perspectives:
  - What perspectives do you see now that you hadn't considered before?
  - What alternative assumptions are emerging?

29 Si and Zhan (2018).

- In light of this reflection, decide which new perspectives and adapted assumptions will become part of your revised mindset. Identify the assumptions you want to let go of entirely.
- Write down the new, adapted core assumption in a few sentences. For example:
  *"I believe/am convinced that*______________________________*"*
  "I am convinced that people want to _________________________*"*
  *"I believe that I have to*____________________ *in order to be successful."*

Transform: Align Behavior and Evaluate Results

The appropriate mindset is tremendously powerful in enhancing your leadership effectiveness during transformation—provided you translate it into observable behavior. Now that you have a clear understanding of your revised mindset, you need to decide which leadership behaviors align most closely with your adapted mindset.

Translate Your Revised Mindset into Leadership Action

Let's return to **Emma** one final time. Her original mindset was rooted in the assumption that leadership skills could not be developed significantly over time and that more *"introverted"* personalities were less capable of leading successfully compared to more *"extroverted"* individuals. This fixed mindset hindered her ability to transform how her team collaborated and to foster flexible leadership among team members. It also prevented her from encouraging the more introverted team members to assume leadership responsibilities actively.

After challenging her assumptions, Emma shifted toward a growth mindset. She began to embrace the idea that—irrespective of their personality preferences—team members could take on leadership responsibilities if she provided them with adequate support and development opportunities.

Emma translates this revised mindset into concrete leadership behaviors. Specifically, she commits herself to:

- conducting individual conversations with each team member, asking about situations where they believe they could take on more leadership responsibility, what they are willing to invest in improving, and what support they would need from Emma and other team members to succeed.
- offering specific opportunities for individual team members, for example to lead meetings with clients, and mentor younger team members during projects.
- monitoring progress over time, ensuring a balanced focus on effort, progress, and results.

- holding regular development and feedback conversations with all team members, leveraging *a* "leader as coach" approach (see ► Chap. 6*)* to foster team members' beliefs in their ability to effectively handle the challenges of assuming greater leadership responsibilities.

Reflect and Act

- How can you translate your adapted mindset into observable behaviors?
- What actions would symbolize your adapted mindset?
- How would others recognize your revised mindset through your behavior?

Evaluate Progress and Guard Against Relapse

Depending on the situation, displaying behavior that differs from your past habits may require courage. It likely won't feel comfortable at first. However, when you assess the results, you may realize that your biggest concerns about your adjusted behavior didn't materialize.

? But what if your adapted behavior doesn't yield the expected outcomes?

One common reason for this is that **we sometimes take a new behavior too far**.

For example, **Emma** may abruptly shift from micromanaging her team to giving them complete freedom to lead specific tasks and work streams without clearly defining responsibilities. This, in turn, may lead to confusion, mistakes, and heightened uncertainty.

By reflecting on these results, Emma can decide how to adjust or refine her behavior so that it better aligns with her revised mindset and her objectives.

To stay on track, you can rely on the same skills that enabled you to shift your mindset.

Use future-focused, transformative questions as a tool to reflect on what changes are needed to ensure your behavior appropriately matches your revised mindset.

Of course, asking team members for feedback can also be a highly valuable source of information.

Reflect and Act

- When would be a good time to test a new behavior that aligns with your adapted mindset? What specific situation could serve as your testing ground?
- How will you evaluate whether this behavior leads to better results in achieving your transformation goals compared to your previous behavior?
- Reflecting on the impact of your adjusted behavior: will you need to further refine it to achieve the positive results you aim for?

Summary

» If you are not ready to change yourself, forget about changing your team and your organization.[30]—Dr. Patrick Liew, executive chairman at GEX Venture

Being aware of your mindset and adapting it to achieve your transformation goals is one of the most powerful tools for effectively leading transformation. This process involves recognizing, challenging, and potentially revising deeply ingrained beliefs, as well as adjusting behavior to align with your revised mindset.

You have now leveraged the ACT process to recognize your current mindset, question its accuracy and completeness, and adapt and transform your mindset to better reflect reality and your transformation goals.

ACKNOWLEDGE To recognize your mindset in relation to a transformation, you

- sharpened your focus and directed your attention toward your thoughts, emotions, and assumptions, catching your thinking in real time.
- accepted your thoughts, emotions, and assumptions as valuable data to work with.
- asked questions to identify your taken-for-granted assumptions.

CHALLENGE To challenge your mindset and its assumptions, you

- adopted a scientist mode, objectively analyzing your mindset.
- used reframing to broaden perspectives and to explore alternative thoughts and assumptions.
- adapted your mindset to better reflect reality and align with your transformation goals.

TRANSFORM To translate your revised mindset into behavior and monitor the results, you

- chose behavior that aligns with your new mindset.
- evaluated the outcomes of this behavior and readjusted it if it didn't yield the desired results.

By adapting and transforming your mindset, you let go of outdated beliefs that might otherwise prevent you from achieving your transformation goals. To successfully initiate and drive significant change, you will also need to help others shift their mindsets which often is an essential prerequisite for others to be able to fully commit to and engage in a transformation.

30 White et al. (2023).

References

Bariso, J. (2017, June 10). Jeff Bezos just revealed 1 thing that sets very smart people apart from the rest. *Inc.com*. https://www.inc.com/justin-bariso/jeff-bezos-just-revealed-1-thing-that-sets-very-smart-people-apart-from-rest.html

Bechara, A., & Damasio, A. R. (2005). The somatic marker hypothesis: A neural theory of economic decision. *Games and Economic Behavior, 52*(2), 336–372. https://doi.org/10.1016/j.geb.2004.06.010

Brassey, J., van Witteloostuijn, A., Huszka, C., Silberzahn, T., & van Dam, N. (2020). Emotional flexibility and general self-efficacy: A pilot training intervention study with knowledge workers. *PLOS ONE, 15*(10), e0237821. https://doi.org/10.1371/journal.pone.0237821

Camuffo, A., Cordova, A., Gambardella, A., & Spina, C. (2019). A scientific approach to entrepreneurial decision-making: Evidence from a randomized control trial. *Management Science, 66*(2), 564–586. https://doi.org/10.1287/mnsc.2018.3249

Colzato, L. S., Ozturk, A., & Hommel, B. (2012). Meditate to create: The impact of focused-attention and open-monitoring training on convergent and divergent thinking. *Frontiers in Psychology, 3*, Article 116. https://doi.org/10.3389/fpsyg.2012.00116

Dweck, C. S. (2017). *Mindset: Changing the way you think to fulfill your potential* (updated ed., Kindle version). Little, Brown Book Group.

Gibbons, P. (2019). *The science of organizational change: How leaders set strategy, change behavior, and create an agile culture* (updated ed., Kindle version). Phronesis Media.

8

Grant, A. (2021). *Think again: The power of knowing what you don't know*. (Kindle version). Viking.

Grecucci, A., Pappaianni, E., Siugzdaite, R., Theuninck, A., & Job, R. (2015). Mindful emotion regulation: Exploring the neurocognitive mechanisms behind mindfulness. *Biomed Research International*. https://doi.org/10.1155/2015/670724

Huang, P. H. (2017). Can practicing mindfulness improve lawyer decision-making, ethics, and leadership? *Houston Law Review, 55*(1), 63–154.

Lazar, S. W., Kerr, C. E., Wasserman, R. H., Gray, J. R., Greve, D. N., Treadway, M. T., McGarvey, M., Quinn, B. T., Dusek, J. A., Benson, H., Rauch, S. L., Moore, C. I., & Fischl, B. (2005). Meditation experience is associated with increased cortical thickness. *NeuroReport, 16*(17), 1893–1897.

Lucas, G. (Director). (1999). *Star Wars: Episode I – The Phantom Menace* [Film]. Lucasfilm.

Miller, K. (2019, December 19). Leadership under pressure: 3 strategies for keeping calm during a crisis. *Harvard Business School Online*. https://online.hbs.edu/blog/post/leadership-under-pressure

Newport, C. (2016). *Deep work: Rules for focused success in a distracted world*. (Kindle version). Grand Central Publishing.

O'Reilly, C. (2024). How Microsoft transformed its culture: Five levers for organizational cultural change. *Management and Business Review, 4*(1), 41–50. https://doi.org/10.1177/26941058202404010006

Oxford University Press. (n.d.). *[Curiosity]*. In *Oxford Learner's Dictionaries*. Retrieved February, 11, 2025, from https://www.oxfordlearnersdictionaries.com/definition/english/[curiosity]

Ren, J., Huang, Z., Luo, J., Wie, G., Ying, X., Ding, Z., Wu, Y., & Luo, F. (2011). Meditation promotes insightful problem-solving by keeping people in a mindful and alert state. *Science China Life Sciences, 54*(10), 961–965. https://doi.org/10.1007/s11427-011-4233-3

Ricard, M., Lutz, A., & Davidson, R. J. (2014, November 1). Neuroscience reveals the secrets of meditation's benefits. *ScientificAmerican*. https://doi.org/10.1038/scientificamerican1114-38

Saïd Business School & EY. (2022). *The future of transformation is human*. University of Oxford. https://www.sbs.ox.ac.uk/sites/default/files/2024-04/ey-the-future-of-transformation-is-human-report.pdf

Si, G., & Zhan, C.-Q. (2018). A Rational Emotive Behavior Therapy (REBT) intervention to improve low frustration tolerance in an elite table tennis player. In M. Turner & R. Bennett (Eds.), *Rational emotive behavior therapy in sport and exercise* (pp. 153–170). Routledge.

Slagter, H. A., Lutz, A., Greischar, L. L., Francis, A. D., Nieuwenhuis, S., Davis, J. M., & Davidson, R. J. (2007). Mental training affects distribution of limited brain resources. *PLOS Biology, 5*(6), e138. https://doi.org/10.1371/journal.pbio.0050138

Tetlock, P. E. (2002). Social functionalist frameworks for judgment and choice: Intuitive politicians, theologians, and prosecutors. *Psychological Review, 109*(3), 451–471. https://doi.org/10.1037/0033-295X.109.3.451

Todesco, C. (2019, February 4). *Entrepreneurs who think like scientists get better results*. Bocconi University. https://www.knowledge.unibocconi.eu/notizia.php?idArt=20337

White, A., Wheelock, M., Canwell, A., & Smets, M. (2023, May 10). 6 Key levers of a successful organizational transformation. *Harvard Business Review*. https://hbr.org/2023/05/6-key-levers-of-a-successful-organizational-transformation

Wittgenstein, L. (1980). *Culture and value*. University of Chicago Press.

Wolińska-Skuza, A. (2022). *The art of changing your mindset: Achieve inner balance and excel in business and life*. (Kindle version). MasConsulting A&B Agnieszka Wolińska-Skuza.

Fueling Exponential Performance Through Multiplier Behaviors

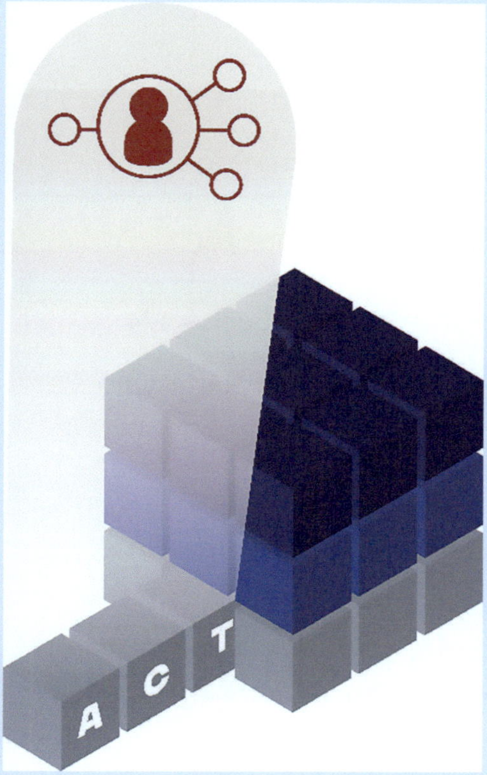

M. Bernhardt, *Leading Transformation in Law Firms*, Law for Professionals,
https://doi.org/10.1007/978-3-031-98653-6_9

Contents

» We judge others by their doings, but ourselves by our intentions.[1]—Edward Wigglesworth

Do You Multiply or Diminish Human Performance in Transformation?

You hire intelligent, capable, and motivated people.

? How much potential might you unintendedly leave untapped?

Despite the growing importance of technology, the human potential for performance that you successfully unleash will likely remain—at least for the foreseeable future—the single most important asset of your firm. Those firms that skillfully tap into this potential will outperform their competitors that fail to do so. This is especially crucial when you are driving significant change within your firm.

According to research by Liz Wiseman, your leadership behavior significantly impacts what potential you actually utilize—or waste.[2] She distinguishes between two types of leaders:

"intelligence multipliers" and **"intelligence diminishers":**[3]

- **Diminishers** underutilize people's talent, skill, and motivation, and leave capability on the table. These leaders, often with the best intentions, limit their firm's potential to thrive during transformation.
- **Multipliers** amplify intelligence, capability, motivation, and ambition, enabling people to contribute to their fullest in a transformation. They leverage human performance optimally.

Naturally, most leaders don't intend to limit others' potential to contribute. Rather, they unintentionally restrict others' opportunities to fully engage.

While the terms "diminisher" and "multiplier" might sound like fixed personality traits, Wiseman focuses on concrete **leadership behaviors** that can inadvertently limit others' potential. Edward Wiggleworth's quote underscores this point: When it comes to others, we focus on what they do—when it comes to ourselves, we often focus on what we meant.

The good news is that diminishing behaviors can change—once leaders recognize their unintended negative impact on others.

Wiseman's research highlights the enormous potential that can be raised:

- Multipliers *"get twice the capacity, plus a growth dividend from their people as their genius expands under the leadership of the Multiplier."*[4]

---

1 Goodreads (n.d.-a) (Wigglesworth).
2 Wiseman (2017) (Kindle version), p. 14 [location 163].
3 Wiseman (2017) (Kindle version), p. 8 [location 98].
4 Wiseman (2017) (Kindle version), p. 82 [location 1044].

- *"Corporations can get 2× more from their resources by turning their most intelligent resources into intelligence Multipliers."*[5]

This raises the question: What are the behavioral differences between leaders who strongly and sustainably boost human performance and those who—often unintendedly—limit it?

Accidental Diminishers: Leaders Who Unintentionally Limit Human Potential

Accidental diminishers are leaders who—despite good intentions—exhibit leadership behaviors that prevent others from fully contributing their talents, skills, and motivation. When these leaders *"walk into a room, the shared IQ drops."*[6]

Whether a behavior actually limits people's potential for performance also depends on the specific situation and context. A behavior that might be effective in one context may hinder performance in another. It is not the behaviors themselves that are "good" or "bad", but rather their influence on people in a given situation.

Thus, you have to take into consideration not only the individuals you lead but also the specific context in which you lead them.

9

When people are confronted with others' diminishing behaviors, they often access only a fraction of their full potential. Gradually, they lose commitment to a transformation. Their confidence shrinks, and their motivation to engage in the transformation diminishes. This threatens the likelihood of achieving the transformation goal you aim for.

? How might diminishing behavior manifest in practice?

Imagine you secretly observe one of your colleagues, **Victor**, the managing partner at a prominent law firm:

Victor is leading a transformation effort to implement a comprehensive digital innovation strategy. His vision includes transitioning to fully digital workflows, adopting advanced case management software, and leveraging artificial intelligence to automate routine legal tasks. Additionally, he aims to integrate generative AI-powered tools to enhance legal research, streamline document review, and improve contract analysis. Beyond efficiency gains, Victor sees generative AI as a strategic enabler that will allow the firm to expand its traditional business model.

Inspired by recent industry trends identified in a recent study on generative AI's impact on law firms,[7] he plans to introduce AI-assisted subscription-based legal services and offer productized legal solutions, moving beyond the traditional bill-

5 Wiseman (2017) (Kindle version), p. 49 [location 629].
6 Wiseman (2017) (Kindle version), p. 22 [location 267].
7 Simon-Kucher & Partners in collaboration with Bucerius Center on the Legal Profession (2025).

able hour model. These innovations will help the firm tap into new client segments and create additional revenue streams.

To succeed, Victor needs full leadership support. The partnership and all senior business services leaders must align with his vision and actively lead their teams through the transformation.

Victor is convinced of the urgent need to drive this transformation to ensure the firm's future-readiness in an industry where technology is reshaping the economics of legal practice.

However, in his view, some business services leaders act too slowly and don't lead this transformation with enough determination. He believes they are capable but just need a little "extra push" to speed things up. Therefore:

- In meetings with business services leaders, Victor frequently intervenes to offer various ideas and solutions, aiming to support brainstorming and accelerate progress.
- To ensure they maintain momentum, he introduces one initiative after another, driven by his desire for business services leaders to move quickly.
- When copied on email chains, he responds at lightning speed to questions—often before the responsible person—hoping to keep things moving.
- Victor never tires of focusing his colleagues on the positives, emphasizing all the opportunities for the firm. He wants them to fully embrace his vision of a resilient, future-ready firm. To sustain enthusiasm, he downplays the inevitable difficulties and frustrations that occur during any transformation.

? The result?

- As Victor floods meetings with ideas, some leaders begin contributing less, and overall creativity in meetings declines.
- By introducing multiple initiatives simultaneously, business services leaders become overwhelmed with too many parallel processes, which leads to mistakes, misunderstandings, and friction.
- As Victor prematurely—and without the necessary information and data—answers emails that are addressed to others, senior leaders feel less accountable for driving the transformation. When Victor realizes that people are getting slower to respond, he intervenes even more frequently which further slows down progress.
- As Victor paints an image of a bright future while completely glossing over any concern, senior leaders don't feel heard with their legitimate reservations in relation to some of Victor's propositions.

? Slowly, some of these talented and capable senior professionals lose their commitment, motivation, and passion to drive the transformation.

Though Victor acts with the best intentions, his behaviors threaten the success of the transformation.

From the outside, the problematic behaviors might seem easy to spot. However, when you are in the midst of leading a transformation, recognizing these patterns can be very challenging. Therefore, becoming aware of your own (and others') typical unintended diminishing behaviors is crucial to drive transformation effectively.

Intentional Multipliers: Leaders Who Deliberately Maximize Potential

Intentional multipliers are leaders who see, utilize, and grow the intelligence, talents, and motivation of others.[8] They enable people to fully access their potential and engage in transformation. These leaders don't just access people's current capabilities but stretch them: *"People actually get smarter and more capable around Multipliers. That is, people don't just feel smarter; they actually become smarter. They can solve harder problems, adapt more quickly, and take more intelligent action."*[9]

A key reason for this is that multipliers **boost people's self-efficacy beliefs**, their confidence that with effort and persistence, they can achieve more than they thought possible.

As a result, people and teams led by "multipliers" are **more productive, innovative, and motivated to contribute** to advancing the firm.

9

To be clear, this approach, as described by Wiseman, has nothing to do with exploiting people or squeezing them like a lemon. Rather, it is about:

- holding very high expectations for everyone.[10]
- recognizing others' potential and believing people can fully realize it.
- trusting in others' ability to learn beyond what they themselves thought possible.
- leading from the stance of a growth mindset (see ► **Chap.** 8).

Together, these factors create a powerful and positive experience for individuals, teams, and ultimately, the entire organization. Multiplying behaviors sustainably build individual's and teams' motivation and performance.

ℹ Most leaders aren't purely "diminishers" or "multipliers"—they tend to display a mix of diminishing and multiplying behavioral tendencies.

Therefore, your goal should not be to free yourself from all potentially diminishing behaviors. Instead, it is essential to focus on those few **behaviors that have an outsized negative impact** and threaten your leadership effectiveness during transformation.

Admittedly, some leaders don't diminish accidentally, but deliberately, because they thrive on other people feeling small, incompetent, and helpless. However,

8 Wiseman (2017) (Kindle version), p. 11 [location 129].
9 Wiseman (2017) (Kindle version), p. 8 [location 91].
10 Wiseman (2017) (Kindle version), p. 7 [location 87].

dealing with these leadership behaviors is an entirely different story and falls outside of the scope of this discussion.

Reflect and Act

Based on your own observations and reflection on how you lead transformation in your firm:

- What multiplying behaviors do you exhibit—helping people and teams perform at their best, stay motivated, and remain engaged even in difficult situations?
- What unintentionally diminishing behaviors might you display—limiting people's and teams' ability to perform at their best?
- Who could provide you with honest, constructive feedback on your leadership behavior?

Leveraging the ACT Process to Unlock Multiplying Behavior

? How can you display more multiplying and fewer diminishing behaviors when leading transformation?

In the first step of the process (ACKNOWLEDGE), you identify typical behaviors that might unintentionally limit others' performance potential. By reflecting on your own leadership behaviors, you analyze the triggers that may contribute to potentially diminishing behaviors.

In the second step (CHALLENGE), you question and shift the assumptions underlying diminishing behaviors that prevent you from changing unhelpful behaviors. Moreover, you select multiplying behaviors that replace former diminishing behaviors—strengthening your positive impact when leading transformation.

Finally, in the third step (TRANSFORM), you establish new behavioral routines to allow for multiplying behaviors to become an integral part of your leadership DNA.

Acknowledge Behavior that Hinders Transformation Success

First, it is important to become more aware of typical diminishing behaviors that may limit effective leadership during a transformation. So, what are these behaviors?

Identify Behavioral Tendencies that May Limit the Potential for Performance

An "unintentionally diminishing behavior" does not automatically have a negative impact on others. **Context plays a critical role** in determining whether a behavior stifles someone's performance potential. As is often the case in leadership, the effect depends on the situation, context, and people involved.

Nonetheless, certain behavioral patterns frequently appear among leaders who unintentionally limit others' ability to perform at their best.

Wiseman identified **nine behavior patterns** that can unintentionally undermine others' performance.[11]

Table 9.1 highlights **five of these nine behavioral patterns**, the ones that, in my experience, are particularly critical for leaders to master during transformation.

Table 9.1 Categories of diminishing behaviors and their negative impact during transformation [Adapted from Wiseman (2017) (Kindle version), p. 246 [location 3197]]

Categories of diminishing behaviors	Leader's good intentions	Unintentionally diminishing behavior	Unintended diminishing impact
Pacesetter	You set high standards for quality and pace to ensure the success of your transformation effort. You are strongly achievement-oriented, lead by example, and expect others to notice and follow your role modeling.	You approach everything you do with high attention to excellent quality and speed, moving at a blistering pace. If you see someone falling behind, you might take over tasks to ensure they meet your high standards. You don't take the time to analyze why someone is *"moving too slowly"*.	People give up because they cannot keep up with your pace. They may become spectators, watching you run from the sidelines. Over time, they might feel less accountable for delivering optimal results.
Idea Fountain	You are creative, have many ideas, and hope to inspire others to generate new ideas themselves when discussing how to move forward during a transformation.	When you—at times prematurely—sense that the free flow of ideas has stopped, you take the lead and offer your ideas, hoping to trigger new thoughts and insights in others. You find it hard to contain your creative impulses and often don't wait until others voice their suggestions.	People stop contributing their own ideas. Instead, they chase yours—either because they find them compelling or because they believe that is what you want. As new ideas keep coming in, people often juggle multiple projects with marginal progress.

(continued)

11 Wiseman (2017) (Kindle version), p. 230 [location 2986].

Table 9.1 (continued)

Categories of diminishing behaviors	Leader's good intentions	Unintentionally diminishing behavior	Unintended diminishing impact
Rapid responder	You want to ensure that people and teams move quickly to achieve transformation goals. You value agility.	When you notice a problem, you solve it immediately. You are quick to act—responding to emails, formulating requests, making decisions, or changing a course of action—even when it is not your responsibility or you lack the required information. You hope others will begin to move as quickly as you do.	People lose commitment as they realize you usually reply faster than they would. They may become frustrated because they have to set things right after you provide insufficient or wrong information. You create so much *"traffic"* that you slow down people who get overwhelmed by the volume of your requests. Rather than fostering agility, you cause stagnation.
Strategist	You are a big thinker and cast a compelling vision, drawing an attractive future and hoping to generate excitement and energy in others. You want to create momentum for the transformation.	As you lay out your vision for the future, you describe it in great detail to ensure others fully visualize it. Rather than letting them come to their own conclusions, you aim to persuade them by being very explicit about the envisioned future.	People don't think through the vision themselves, including its inevitable challenges and how to overcome them. They second-guess what you want them to do and seek your guidance instead of taking the lead.
Optimist	You trust in people's capabilities and believe they can achieve the designated transformation goals, even during significant challenges.	You hope to inspire people to *"aim for the stars"* and rise to the transformation challenges. You maintain an optimistic outlook and display a *"can-do"* attitude, regardless of the obstacles.	People don't feel heard or understood in their struggles and concerns. They believe you brush aside the possibility of failure too quickly. The more you emphasize the positives, the more they insist you are overlooking difficulties.

As noted earlier, having any of these behavioral tendencies does not inevitably limit others' abilities to engage in a transformation. However, these tendencies increase the likelihood of a negative impact on transformation success.

Recognize Individual Limiting Behaviors and Their Triggers

❓ Which diminishing tendencies might you recognize in yourself during a transformation?

Moving from diminisher to multiplier behaviors starts with understanding whether you display any unintentionally diminishing behaviors and how they impact others' capacities to drive a transformation effort.

Recognizing the adverse effects of your behavior on others isn't as easy as it might seem. Wiseman points out that *"when you have a diminishing impact, you are likely to be completely unaware of it and probably the last to know."*[12]

Therefore, if you are unsure, it may be helpful to **seek feedback** from a trusted colleague. It is in the nature of things that others are often better at recognizing our blind spots. **Asking your colleague** some of the following questions can shed light on your behaviors that might limit others' performance:

- Despite my best intentions, how might I be shutting down the ideas and actions of others during a transformation?
- What do you see me doing that could have a negative impact on others, limiting their potential to fully contribute to a transformation? For example: Am I monopolizing discussions, not allowing others enough space to contribute? Am I behaving in a way that undermines others' confidence or restricts their creative input?. Do my actions inadvertently discourage others from taking responsibility, making decisions, or thinking problems through?
- In your view, what is one thing I could do differently to significantly improve my positive impact on others, enabling them to engage in and contribute to the success of a transformation?

❓ What triggers diminishing behaviors for you?

A trigger can be any event, situation, or person that immediately:

- activates specific thoughts about the situation or person, and how to achieve the transformation goal—based on your mindset and core assumptions;
- causes you to experience strong emotions such as irritation, anger, or fear; and
- leads you to react quickly, without previous reflection.

Typically, when you feel triggered, you react as if on **autopilot**—quickly and without consciously considering the potential consequences of your behavior.

Acting on autopilot can be helpful in situations that require immediate responses. However, this response pattern is less helpful when it causes you to display diminishing behaviors.

12 Wiseman (2017) (Kindle version), p. 240 [location 3124].

? How can you effectively deal with these triggers and consciously choose behaviors that support the transformation?

First, it is necessary to understand what triggers your diminishing behaviors.

To do so, you need to **recognize in real time** when you have been triggered. The quicker you notice this, the easier it will be to deliberately decide how to respond, rather than reacting impulsively.

To improve your ability to identify triggers and spot diminishing tendencies as they occur, you can use techniques that enhance focus and attention (see ▶ **Chap.** 8 on "attention focus training" and mindfulness practices). With practice, you will recognize in real time when you are being triggered.

As we will see in the next step (CHALLENGE), instead of giving in to the impulse, you can intentionally select a "multiplying" behavior that helps others unleash their potential.

Challenge: Shift from Diminishing Behaviors to Multiplying Practices

Confront Destructive Behaviors and Reframe Unhelpful Assumptions

? What behaviors do you currently display that limit your positive impact on other people's performance, motivation, and commitment during transformation?

Concentrate on just one or two behavioral patterns that—if you succeeded in shifting them to be more "multiplying"—could have a significant positive effect on others and a successful transformation outcome.

Reflect and Act

- What are your diminishing behaviors that limit others' ability to fully contribute to transformation and that ultimately hinder the success of the envisioned change?

	Pace-setter	Idea fountain	Rapid responder	Strate-gist	Opti-mist	Other behavior
That is me!						
This happens at times						
Not my style						

- What concrete behavior do you commit to improving, starting immediately?

	Pace-setter	Idea fountain	Rapid responder	Strat-egist	Opti-mist	Other behavior
I want to work on that one						

Often, behavior follows assumptions.

We act the way we do because we believe it is the best way to achieve our goals.

Thus, to transform destructive behavior, it is essential to **be aware of the underlying assumptions—your mindset—that drive your current behavior**.

Once you understand the assumptions you make, you can start adapting them to inspire and enable others to fully engage in a transformation (see ▶ **Chap.** 8 on how to shift your assumptions).

These are two typical assumptions that reflect diminishing behaviors:

- I need to push people to their extremes for them to perform at their highest level.
- Without my guidance, people won't be able to figure this out.

Here are two typical assumptions that reflect multiplying behaviors:

- People have the smarts to figure it out.
- People are skilled; they want and can fully contribute to our transformation goal.

The latter two assumptions may remind you of the growth mindset, covered in ▶ **Chap.** 8.

Indeed, **the growth mindset forms the foundation for many multiplying behaviors**. Thus, one option to foster multiplying behavior is to adapt the assumptions that currently drive your diminishing tendencies by shifting them toward a growth mindset.

Reflect and Act

Take a look at the diminishing behaviors you have identified so far:

- What assumptions are you making that lead to you showing these exact behaviors?
- What alternative assumptions could you embrace to show more multiplying behaviors?

Lead with Intention: Chose Practices that Multiply Human Performance

By now, you have identified how your behaviors might negatively impact others' ability to reach their full potential during a transformation. You understand the specific triggers—people, events, or situations—that lead you to display these behaviors. You have committed to focusing on a few key diminishing behaviors and adjusting them to become multiplying behaviors. You have examined the role of your assumptions and, if necessary, begun to adapt them to embrace more of a growth mindset.

Multiplying practices, as described by Wiseman, can help you transition from diminishing to multiplying behaviors.

Table 9.2 presents multiplying practices that enable you to unlock potential. For more details on these practices, please refer to Wiseman (2017).[13]

Table 9.2 Multiplying practices that help people and teams fully leverage their potential

Category	Leading with intention	Multiplying practices
Pacesetter	Make sure you stay connected with people. Figuratively speaking, stay within sight so that you notice when they lose speed and need your support to catch up.	*"One size too big"* *"Acknowledge your faults"*
Idea Fountain	Before sharing your thoughts and ideas, ensure you give others enough time to voice theirs.	*"Questions only"* *"Create a debate"*
Rapid responder	Know your triggers and establish a mandatory waiting period before reacting to them, such as responding to emails that fall within someone else's domain.	*"Questions only"* *"Create a debate"*
Strategist	When describing your vision for the future, focus on the *"why"* and *"what"*. Leave room for others to define the *"how"*, allowing them to determine how the transformation can be achieved.	*"Questions only"* *"Play fewer chips"*
Optimist	Acknowledge struggles, setbacks, and failures. Recognize that transformation is challenging and that success isn't a given.	*"Make space for mistakes"* *"Create a debate"*

13 Wiseman (2017) (Kindle version), p. 404 [location 5062].

Multiplying practices consist of specific actions that reinforce multiplying behaviors. Based on Wiseman's research,[14] here are some—slightly adapted—examples of how multiplying practices can enhance your positive impact:

- **Play Fewer Chips**

You decide on a specific number of "poker chips" (e.g., five) for your next meeting. You limit the number of your contributions to the number of poker chips. Once you have used all your chips—mentally or physically—you stop contributing, except for listening or asking open-ended questions.

This exercise is extremely powerful for several reasons:

- You become more aware of how frequently you contribute in a typical meeting.
- You become more deliberate about when to speak and what to say/ask.
- You allow yourself to observe how a meeting unfolds when you intervene less.
- You create space for yourself to listen more to others.

- **Questions Only**

You leverage open-ended questions to elicit ideas and suggestions in discussions. You use different types of questions to help others to:

- change perspectives
- voice ideas, questions, or concerns
- challenge assumptions
- advance discovery when addressing problems.

You can combine this practice with "Play fewer chips". In that case, every time you give a comment, offer advice, or speak in any other way, it costs you a poker chip.

- **One Size Too Big**

You support an employee by giving them a stretch assignment that enables them to develop specific skills during a transformation. To achieve this, you use your skills as a "leader-as-coach" (see ▶ **Chap.** 6) to systematically guide the person with open-ended questions, deepening their reflection and learning. You resist the urge to take over the task yourself.

- **Create a Debate**

When you face an important decision and want to encourage a discussion where everyone can contribute, begin by framing the issue: What is the question? Why does it matter? And how will the decision be made?

After this, you facilitate the debate by encouraging diverse viewpoints, helping people shift perspectives, and sharing your thoughts last.

---

14 Adapted from Wiseman (2017) (Kindle version), p. 368 [location 4650].

Make Space for Mistakes

You explain where experimentation is necessary to drive transformation, where potential mistakes are factored in, and where boundaries for experimentation must be set. This ensures that people understand which mistakes are acceptable under specific conditions and which mistakes could jeopardize the transformation's success or compromise important values, such as the firm's reputation.

To help individuals and teams distinguish between types of mistakes, you can draw on Amy Edmondson's distinction among preventable, complex, and intelligent failures[15] (see ▶ **Chap.** 5). While preventable failures—as the term suggests—should be avoided, intelligent failures occur when exploring uncharted territories and should be encouraged in situations where learning opportunities are high and new insights crucial.

Acknowledge Your Faults

When you want to model the value of experimentation and learning, you can share stories about your own mistakes. Reflect on your career to identify the mistakes you learned from the most. Look for opportunities to share one of these stories with someone who might benefit from viewing mistakes as a chance for learning and growth.

Reflect and Act

Consider the diminishing behaviors you aim to address:
- Which of the described multiplying practices could be most helpful?
- What additional actions might have a positive, multiplying effect on others?
- What is one practice you can commit to implementing, starting today?

To fully benefit from the power of multiplying practices, it is essential that they take place in a climate of mutual trust and **psychological safety** (see ▶ **Chap.** 5). Psychological safety is the belief that the context is safe for interpersonal risk taking[16]—that speaking up with ideas, questions, concerns, or mistakes will be welcomed and valued. It creates the environment teams need to fully benefit from multiplying practices.

Transform: Close the Knowing-Doing Gap

> If you're having trouble changing your habits, the problem isn't you. The problem is your system. Bad habits repeat themselves again and again not because you don't want to change, but because you have the wrong system for change.[17]—James Clear

15 Edmondson (2023) (Kindle version), p. 32, location [480].
16 Edmondson (1999).
17 Clear (2018) (Kindle version), p. 27 [location 418].

Develop Multiplier Habits to Lead Transformation Effectively

A habit is *"a routine or behavior that is performed regularly—and, in many cases, automatically."*[18] You can think of a habit as a shortcut for repeating actions that worked for you in the past and provided some reward.[19]

When you consistently exhibit a diminishing behavior, it has become a habit—one that is triggered either by external factors, such as a specific situation, a person, or internal factors, such as your mindset and assumptions.

? What does it take to move from potentially diminishing behavioral tendencies to multiplying behaviors?

Make the New Habit Obvious

In his insightful book, James Clear describes small, specific actions that help establish new habits.[20]

The first essential step is to **make the new habit obvious**. You achieve this by designing your environment to include visible cues or triggers that prompt your desired behavior.

Ask yourself, *"What triggers my current diminishing behavior?"* **Identify the specific situations or moments where you tend to display diminishing behaviors**, such as being an "idea fountain", offering too many suggestions or solutions. Meetings with your team, brainstorming sessions, or interactions where team members seek your advice might trigger your current diminishing behaviors. Thus, each of these instances presents an opportunity to implement a new habit.

Select one specific situation that in your view is best suited for testing a new habit.

First, identify the **concrete circumstances** within that situation that lead to the behavior. For instance, it may not be the meeting itself that prompts diminishing behavior, but rather the fact that you have rushed from one meeting to the next all day without a break, even to drink a glass of water, depleting your cognitive resources and making impulse control more difficult.

Second, ask yourself how you could **tweak your environment** a little bit—in this case to remind yourself to drink enough water.

Third, create **new visual cues** to remind yourself of the new habit you want to establish. These could include visual reminders, such as poker chips, a motivational quote on a postcard on your desk, or digital notifications. These cues ensure that the trigger for your new habit is always in plain sight, reducing the risk of overlooking it.

18 Clear (2018) (Kindle version), p. 6 [location 137].
19 Wood and Barnett (2019).
20 Clear (2018).

By **designing your environment to include clear signals**, you increase the likelihood of adopting your desired multiplying behavior.

Reflect and Act

- What does currently trigger your diminishing habit?
- What cues might help you create a multiplying habit in that situation?

Make the New Habit Easy

» The best is the enemy of the good.[21]—Voltaire

Simplifying the process of habit formation is crucial for consistency. Therefore, to make the new habit easy to display, break it down into small, manageable steps that can be easily integrated into your routine.

Your goal is to implement a new habit sustainably, so that it becomes automatic with repetition. For this to happen, **take action quickly** instead of planning for too long. As Voltaire pointedly observed, striving for perfection can prevent achieving good or satisfactory results.

ⓘ One effective technique is **habit stacking**: You link a new habit to an existing one using the formula: *"After [current habit that you already use], I will [new habit]."*

For example: *"After I open my notebook or meeting notes at the beginning of a meeting [current habit], I will pour myself a glass of water before starting the discussion [new habit]."*

Or: *"After I open my notebook or meeting notes at the beginning of a meeting [current habit], I will ask an open-ended question to start the discussion and then listen attentively [new habit]."*

Reflect and Act

- How can you use habit stacking to make your new habit easier to implement?
- Write down your concrete commitment:
  "After ……, I …."

21 Goodreads (n.d.-b) (Voltaire).

Reinforce the New Habit

As humans, we all have a preference for instant gratification: "*What is immediately rewarded is repeated. What is immediately punished is avoided.*"[22]

When a satisfying outcome follows each instance of the new behavior, it creates a positive feedback loop that increases the chances of the behavior becoming a habit.

Thus, to retain and reinforce a new habit, it should yield **immediate and tangible rewards**. Simply put, you will want to repeat a behavior if it feels satisfying and not painful.

For example, **track your progress** in a journal. Note each meeting where you successfully "play fewer poker chips". Cross off each day you display the new behavior. Over time, your brain craves the reward of crossing off another day, motivating you to continue.

Reflect and Act

- How can you track progress to support your new habit consistently?
- Who could provide you with feedback on your progress?
- How will you ensure that you set aside time for reflection to evaluate your progress and make necessary adjustments?
- How can you celebrate small wins along the way?

? How long does it take to form a new habit?

Research suggests that forming a simple habit can take up to 2–3 months.[23] However, the sheer number of days isn't what matters most. Instead, it is the **frequency with which you perform the new habit**. So, aim for as much frequency as possible. In other words: practice, practice, practice.

Summary

You have now acquired the tools to transition from accidentally diminishing to intentionally multiplying behaviors to fully unlock others' potential for performance during a transformation.

You have leveraged the ACT process to understand the implications of diminishing versus multiplying leadership behavior in transformations. You have identified the triggers that lead to potentially diminishing behaviors, challenged their

22 Clear (2018) (Kindle version), p. 186 [location 2392].
23 Lally et al. (2010) and Wood and Barnett (2019).

validity, and adapted your behavior to form new habits that empower others to fully contribute during transformation.

ACKNOWLEDGE To acknowledge unintentionally diminishing behavior, you

- identified typical diminishing behaviors that can inadvertently limit others' performance.
- recognized your individual diminishing tendencies that may prevent others from fully contributing to a transformation, thereby hindering success.
- analyzed the external and internal triggers that currently cause you to exhibit unintentional diminishing behaviors.

CHALLENGE To challenge diminishing tendencies, you

- focused on potentially diminishing behaviors that could have a significant negative impact on your ability to successfully drive transformation.
- uncovered and questioned unhelpful assumptions, shifting them to support easier adoption of multiplying behaviors.
- selected multiplying practices to counter diminishing tendencies.

TRANSFORM To transition toward multiplying instead of diminishing leadership behaviors, you

- established new habits by making them obvious, easy, and likely to be repeated.
- tracked progress and evaluated the results, making further adjustments as needed.

References

Clear, J. (2018). *Atomic habits: An easy & proven way to build good habits & break bad ones* (Kindle version), p. 27 [location 418]. Random House.

Edmondson, A. C. (1999). Psychological safety and learning behavior in work teams. *Administrative Science Quarterly, 44*(2), 350–383. https://doi.org/10.2307/2666999

Edmondson, A. C. (2023). *Right kind of wrong: The science of failing well.* (Kindle version). Simon & Schuster.

Goodreads. (n.d.-a) (Wigglesworth). *Quote by Edward Wigglesworth.* Retrieved February 12, 2025, from https://www.goodreads.com/quotes/8896744-we-judge-others-by-their-doings-but-ourselves-by-our

Goodreads. (n.d.-b) (Voltaire). Quote by Voltaire: "Le mieux est l'ennemi du bien. (The perfect is the..." [Quote]. *Goodreads.* Retrieved February 12, 2025, from https://www.goodreads.com/quotes/215866-le-mieux-est-l-ennemi-du-bien-the-perfect-is-the

Lally, P., van Jaarsveld, C. H. M., Potts, H. W. W., & Wardle, J. (2010). How are habits formed: Modelling habit formation in the real world. *European Journal of Social Psychology, 40*(6), 998–1009. https://doi.org/10.1002/ejsp.674

Simon-Kucher & Partners in collaboration with Bucerius Center on the Legal Profession. (2025). *The AI-Conomics of Legal Services. How generative AI will transform the commercial model of law.*

Wiseman, L. (2017). *Multipliers: How the best leaders make everyone smarter* (rev. ed., Kindle version). HarperCollins.

Wood, W., & Barnett, M. (2019, October 14). Good habits, bad habits: A conversation with Wendy Wood. *Behavioral Scientist*. https://behavioralscientist.org/good-habits-bad-habits-a-conversation-with-wendy-wood/

Uncovering Hidden Competing Goals to Empower Personal Transformation

M. Bernhardt, *Leading Transformation in Law Firms*, Law for Professionals,
https://doi.org/10.1007/978-3-031-98653-6_10

Contents

» The measure of intelligence is the ability to change.—***Albert Einstein***

"What is holding me back?" Martin wonders. *"I know I have to write these invoices. This is how our business works. Why am I just not doing it?"*

It is December, 21st, and Martin has just returned from an unpleasant conversation with his COO, Jenna, who, for the fourth time, reminded him about the €650,000 in **outstanding bills he has yet to invoice**.

In a way, Martin admired Jenna: Like an elephant, she never forgot anything, and like a terrier, she never let her prey off the hook. Only that this time, obviously he was her prey.

Martin felt like a 7-year-old schoolboy when he tried to explain to her what he couldn't even explain to himself. Gosh, how he dreaded invoicing. Just thinking about it made his energy levels plummet into a bottomless abyss. He simply couldn't bring himself to write invoices. It was absurd, almost as if an invisible force was holding him back from even going there.

Despite his workload as a newly appointed Managing Partner, Martin had managed to maintain and even grow his client base. In fact, he was one of the highest-performing partners in the firm. That used to make him proud. If only it weren't for the relentless pressure to bill, which had significantly intensified since he took on his new role.

Jenna had made Martin promise to invoice by Dec. 23rd, and he knew she wouldn't let him get away with blithely ignoring his problem this time.

He had to change his behavior for good if he wanted to maintain credibility as a responsible and capable partner and as a Managing Partner, not just with Jenna but also with his fellow partners, who were increasingly bemused by his unwillingness—or inability—to follow the firm's rules on timely invoicing.

Especially with all the significant changes and transformations in the firm, he was asking his peers' support for, he needed to set the right example. After all, how could he expect his peers to shift their leadership behaviors, for example, spending more time developing employees, if he couldn't even bring himself to write those accursed invoices?

Martin is determined to change his behavior for good. He believes he has the will and the skills to do so. And yet, he catches himself thinking, *"But then again, I have been determined to develop an efficient and effective billing routine many times before, but in all honesty, I haven't changed much."*

No Organizational Transformation Without Personal Transformation

Right now, you might wonder, *"Seriously? This seems like a rather small goal. Are we really talking about transformation goals here? Martin, get your act together and do it. Full stop."*

Indeed, at first glance, this challenge might seem trivial. But let's use this simple example to explore the deeper psychological dynamics behind the *"resistance"* to personal transformation and how to overcome this *"resistance"* sustainably.

Why does this matter?

Because to skillfully lead any kind of transformation in your firm, you, too, will likely need to change certain behaviors and patterns of thinking that made you successful in the past but no longer serve you. In all these cases, as Albert Einstein's quote suggests, intelligence lies in our ability to adapt and change.

For example, maybe:

- you need to adopt a different leadership style than was required in the past, as the ability to effectively lead cross-functional teams has become increasingly pivotal.
- your area of responsibility has expanded, and you must delegate many tasks you used to handle yourself.
- you have repeatedly received feedback that a behavior you see as empowering is actually hindering your team's development and growth—making it necessary for you to change this behavior (see ▶ **Chap.** 9 on multiplying leadership behaviors).

If you genuinely want to change a behavior but do not succeed over a longer period, it may not be because you are unwilling, incapable, or actively resisting change. Instead, a subconscious, hidden psychological dynamic may prevent you from acting in a way that enables sustainable behavior change.

Robert Kegan and Lisa Lahey from Harvard Business School call this hidden force "immunity to change."[1]

Their research highlights the crucial impact of these hidden dynamics on individual and team performance, and, ultimately, on the entire firm.

Kegan et al. (2014) emphasize that *"most people at work, even* ***in high-performing organizations****, divert considerable energy every day to a second job that no one has hired them to do: preserving their reputations, putting their best selves forward, and hiding their inadequacies from others and themselves. We believe* ***this is the single biggest cause of wasted resources in nearly every company today****."*[2]

To help leaders uncover and overcome this barrier, Kegan and Lahey developed a structured approach designed to **reveal the underlying mechanisms that hold people back**.

Mastering these skills is essential for you to be as effective a leader as possible:

In many transformations, you are asking a lot from others. They may need to embrace more risk, collaborate in ways they are not used to, learn new skills, or unlearn habits that once made them successful. If you effectively adapt your behavior—and corresponding mindset—you will be a role model for everyone you expect to do the same. You will demonstrate what it looks like to navigate a personal transformation.

---

1 Kegan and Lahey (2001), p. 85; Kegan and Lahey (2009).
2 Kegan et al. (2014), p. 45 [emphasis added].

If you are unable to change a behavior that hinders your effectiveness, it will be much harder to ask others to adapt theirs to enable transformation in your firm. After all:

? If you can't change your behavior, how will you credibly lead small or large-scale transformation projects that require others to change theirs?

Moreover, once you know how to sustainably change your own behavior, you can **apply these skills to help others**, peers and employees, successfully shift their behaviors and mindsets as well.

Supporting others in their personal transformation is a critical leadership skill and a powerful way to drive transformation successfully across the firm.

Leveraging the ACT Process to Overcome "Resistance" to Change

The ACT process helps you overcome struggles with behavior change. By unlocking personal transformation, you can act in ways that align with your transformation goals.

In the first step (ACKNOWLEDGE), you define your goal, and identify the behaviors that unwittingly undermine goal achievement. You uncover the underlying reasons for your current behavior, including unquestioned beliefs that may subconsciously influence your behavior.

In the second step of the process (CHALLENGE), you question these assumptions and analyze their rationale. You begin to shift the core beliefs that prevent you from successfully changing behavior.

Finally (TRANSFORM), you test new behaviors that are aligned with your goal, evaluate the outcome, and further adapt behavior if needed.

Acknowledge Root Causes for "Resistance" to Shift Behavior

Let's assume Martin has asked you—a highly respected colleague, trusted and empathetic friend to be his peer coach in his quest to transform his behavior.

As it happens, you have just learned about a powerful tool—the **"immunity-to-change" framework**—that can help Martin overcome his personal transformation inertia.

i The immunity-to-change framework is a structured approach that helps uncover hidden dynamics that prevent effective behavior change.

It leads individuals through a series of reflective questions:

- What is your **goal**—your primary commitment? What do you want to change, and why?
- What **behaviors** hold you back and work against your goal?

- What **competing goals**—competing commitments—fuel these behaviors that work against your goal?
- What **assumptions** support these competing goals and lead you to continue behaving the same way?
- How can you **test** these assumptions?

The **framework can be applied to groups, teams, and even entire partnerships** that feel stuck despite their commitment to change. However, in this context, we focus entirely on individual behavior change.

In Our Scenario you are ready to help Martin get out of his own way and shift his behavior.

You will lead Martin through the framework, prompting reflection with a structured sequence of questions.

Identify Your Goal and Behaviors that Hold You Back

You kick off the coaching session with a simple question:

› "Martin, what is the goal you want to reach with my help?"

When asked what his goal—or "primary commitment"—is, Martin replies without hesitation, *"I want to invoice all the work I do for my clients regularly and timely. My goal is to create a sustainable invoicing habit. I want to prove that I can personally transform. If I can do it, my peers can do it as well. They, too, can change the behaviors they exhibit that limit performance—whether their own, others' or the firm's."*

This is pretty straightforward, and Martin's determination is palpable.

Reflect and Act

Think about a behavior you have wanted to change for a long time—without visible progress so far—and that prevents you from achieving a transformation-related goal in your firm.

For example, you may have wanted to:

- delegate more tasks to free up time for the strategic development of your firm—but so far, you haven't.
- increase structured feedback conversations to help your team develop and advance their ability to drive change—but so far, you haven't given more feedback.
- schedule time each week to immerse yourself in selected artificial intelligence tools so you can role-model learning in your organization—but you keep postponing it.
- Write down the specific behavior you want to change.

- What will it look like when you have successfully changed the behavior?
- This is your **goal**—or **primary commitment**—you have promised yourself to reach.
- On a scale from **one** to **ten**, how much do you want to reach this goal?

1	2	3	4	5	6	7	8	9	10
Reflecting on it now, in all honesty, I do not want to reach it.									*I would be ready to do whatever it takes to finally reach that goal.*

If your answer is below **six**, ask yourself candidly: Is this goal truly worth your time and energy? Behavior change is simple in theory but difficult in practice. Developing a new habit takes discipline, frustration tolerance, and stamina. If this goal doesn't feel important enough, consider choosing one that scores higher and holds a greater value for you and your firm.

As Martin hasn't reached his goal yet, he is probably not behaving in a way that facilitates goal attainment. You ask him:

"All right, if this is your goal, then what exactly are you doing—or omitting to do—that is keeping you from achieving it?"

Martin pauses to think and—with an apologetic smile—answers:

» *To be honest, I have not invoiced significant bills in the past.* ***I often wait until the last minute****. Then, I mainly invoice what I believe would be most embarrassing for me if others found out.* ***I do not structure and manage the billing*** *in a way that would make it easier for me to do it.* ***I don't regularly dedicate time to the process****. I only act when I have my back against the wall, when I can no longer avoid discussions with my COO and peers, or when unnerved clients call. I am still considered a successful partner despite this, but only because I have so many high-volume mandates that, as long as I invoice some of them, the numbers still work out.* ***I have become a tragic "master of failed-to-bill excuses"*** *of all kinds, even fabricating relatives' illnesses to justify my delays. I am not proud to admit that. And even now, with Jenna breathing down my neck, I catch myself thinking about potential excuses instead of just getting the billing done.*

You just helped Martin articulate the ***behaviors*** that hinder his personal transformation.

These behaviors also likely prevent him from successfully driving larger transformations in the firm—transformations that require his fellow partners to change their behavior as well. If he cannot even change a seemingly minor habit, such as timely invoicing, how can he credibly expect others to make far more significant shifts?

Reflect and Act

Take a moment to reflect on your leadership behaviors in relation to the specified goal:

- Which behaviors are preventing you from successfully achieving the goal you identified above?
- What specific things do you do—or fail to do—that keep you from making progress and reaching your goal?

Uncover Hidden Competing Goals and Their Rationale

As Martin's peer coach, you recognize there must be a valid **reason for the discrepancy** between Martin's stated goal (to invoice regularly) and his contradictory behavior.

You ask:

"Martin, what are your concerns? What do you fear might happen if you fully focused on reaching your change goal and took decisive action to invoice regularly and on time?"

Martin explains:

> *I worry that administrative tasks—like billing—will consume my time and distract me from practicing law, which I love and excel at. As a Managing Partner, I already handle a lot of admin work, and it is draining. I don't want it to interfere with my client focus. My joy and satisfaction come from serving clients, and invoicing threatens that. While I accept that some unpleasant tasks are part of my role, working with clients makes me genuinely happy and I want to keep it that way. Besides, if I got better at admin work, I would end up with an even heavier load—my worst nightmare. At the moment, my COO and colleagues shield me from these tasks, and I'd like it to stay that way.*

You share your thoughts with Martin:

> Listening to your reflection, I assume that you have committed yourself to ensuring that these concerns don't materialize. In light of this commitment, it makes sense that you avoid writing invoices and instead prioritize client work. Looking again at the concerns you just described, what exactly have you committed yourself to doing?

Martin reflects:

> *Well, considering the concerns I mentioned, I guess* ***I am committed to devoting as much energy and time as possible to the substantive legal work my clients need****—rather than administrative tasks like billing. I am also* ***committed to deriving satisfaction from working with my clients.*** *For me, joyful experiences come from the insights I gain and the insights I enable my clients to have. And I am also* ***committed, in my role as Managing Partner, to focusing as much as possible on the substantive aspects of the initiatives*** *I want to drive. For me, this means keeping anything unrelated at bay—especially getting lost in administrative work.*

Together, you have uncovered Martin's **competing goals**—or **competing commitments**.

These subconscious competing goals drive Martin's current behavior—the same behavior that undermines his primary commitment to invoice regularly. When viewed through this lens, the inconsistency between Martin's stated goal and his contradictory behavior is no longer irrational. In fact, it makes perfect sense.

Reflect and Act

- What concerns do you have about fully committing to your stated change goal and taking decisive action to achieve it?
- What underlying commitments might be driving you to continue your current behavior?

Challenge the Big Assumption that Fuels "Resistance" to Change

You and Martin have now defined Martin's primary goal, identified his counterproductive behaviors, and uncovered the competing commitments that drive them.

For Martin to successfully change his behavior, he must get to the root cause of his behavior, fully understanding **why his competing commitments are so strong**.

These root causes often consist of deeply held beliefs about oneself, others, and the world at large—beliefs that are typically never questioned for their accuracy.

ⓘ These unquestioned, subconscious beliefs are a person's **big assumptions**.[3]

3 Kegan and Lahey (2001), p. 88.

A big assumption strengthens the power of competing commitments, causing you to hold on to counterproductive behaviors. Unconsciously, you behave in ways that protect and sustain your big assumption.

We often develop big assumptions at an early age or during our legal education and professional socialization. Even when they no longer serve us, we unconsciously hold on to them. The result is mental and behavioral patterns that can significantly impair our capacity to change and transform.

Over time, this immunity to change can undermine organization-wide transformation efforts.

Unmask Your Big Assumption: Flesh Out Your Worst-Case Scenario

Let's take a closer look at what Martin believes deep down:

You ask:

- "Martin, what do you fear could happen if you behaved in a way that allowed you to change and invoice regularly and on time?"

Martin hesitates, then starts:

» As I already said, I assume that if I prioritized invoicing more, I would have **less time and energy to work on the substantive client matters**. And I would probably **have to take on even more administrative tasks as a Managing Partner**.

» You: "And if that happened, then what?"
Martin: "I would **lose the joy** I get from focusing on a case."

» You: "And if that happened, what would be the result?"
Martin: "I'd become **less creative and engaged**, and the **quality of my work would drop**."

» You: "And then what?"
Martin: "Clients would be **dissatisfied** with my results."

» You: "And if that happened, then what?"
Martin: "They'd eventually **stop hiring** me."

» You: "And if that happened, what would be the result?"
Martin: "Word would get around, and **my peers would think** that I can't handle being a successful partner and Managing Partner."

» You: "And what would happen then?"
Martin: "I would **lose credibility**, and it would be much harder to advance the projects I care about or drive transformation across the firm."

» You: "And if that happened, what would be the result?"
Martin: "Ultimately, I'd have to **step down as Managing Partner**... and maybe even leave the firm, having failed my peers."

This is Martin's big assumption:

» If I devote more attention to administrative tasks such as invoicing, ultimately, I risk compromising my effectiveness as a partner and as a leader driving transformation. If that happens, I may even have to step down.

As Martin's coach, you may find yourself thinking:

» Come on, Martin, are you serious? This is clearly over the top and highly unlikely to happen.

Indeed, from an **outside perspective**, it is easy to dismiss Martin's fears as unrealistic or exaggerated. But if **catastrophizing** was entirely rational, you wouldn't call it that; it would simply be a realistic prediction.

However, for Martin, this scenario **feels** real. If his concerns and accompanying emotions weren't so powerful, they wouldn't influence his behavior so strongly.

Reflect and Act

Imagine behaving in a way that moves you closer to your stated goal and successfully changing your behavior:

- What do you fear might happen if you took the actions necessary to achieve this change?
- What would happen then? And then what?
- At your core, what do you believe would ultimately happen if you fully aligned your behavior with your goal?

This is your big assumption.

Rethink Your Big Assumption: Reframe It to Unlock Change

By now, it has become clear that Martin will not make progress toward his goal to change his behavior and establish a sustainable invoicing routine—at least not unless he challenges the **validity** of his big assumption.

Not every big assumption is entirely wrong. Often, these assumptions contain a grain of truth, which is what makes them so powerful and deceptive.

Most of the time, however, they are not as absolute as they claim to be.

Unless we question the accuracy of our big assumption, it is difficult to achieve lasting behavior change because that change would contradict a deeply held belief.

Typically, adapting behavior and shifting assumptions go hand in hand.
You explain to Martin:

» As long as your big assumption remains unchallenged, you will continue seeing the world through this lens. This makes you prone to **confirmation bias**: Instinctively, you will overvalue anything that supports your big assumption and dismiss anything that contradicts it.

Whenever your new invoicing behavior leads to seemingly negative outcomes, your big assumption will become even more ingrained. You won't stick to any new invoicing habit for long. Instead, you will tell yourself, 'See? I knew invoicing would lead to harmful results.'

Through a series of targeted questions, you help Martin break down the components of his big assumption, identify what makes behavior change difficult for him, and distill options to overcome these barriers:

■ Transitioning from Partner to Managing Partner May Require Shifting to a Systemic Perspective

When asked to consider invoicing from a Managing Partner's leadership perspective, Martin realizes that his subject-matter focus, which once made him successful, is now limiting his **broader responsibilities**.

He also sees that he isn't the only one struggling with invoicing, and **the firm's continued growth requires a much more structured, efficient billing process**.

Instead of asking himself, *"How do I ensure I invoice on time?"*, Martin reframes the question: *"What firm-wide process, possibly automated, will achieve the best results in terms of effectiveness, efficiency, cash flow, and service quality?"*

10

By reframing invoicing from a low-value chore into a high-value strategic priority, Martin shifts his mindset.

Martin adopts a **systemic perspective** and initiates a discussion on how to design an automated invoicing process, then delegates its development.

Rather than being at risk of losing credibility as Managing Partner, and potentially even having to step down, Martin is now actively driving a strategic solution that strengthens the firm's financial health.

■ Fully Embracing the Role of Managing Partner May Mean Letting Go of Cherished Tasks

You ask Martin: *"What do you need to **stop doing** in the future to be successful as Managing Partner?"*

This question forces Martin to confront an uncomfortable reality: he cannot continue working in the exact same way he did before.

As painful as it is, he will have to start delegating some client work to other partners to be the Managing Partner he set out to be. His success as a leader depends on his ability to shift his focus more fully from personal client work to the firm's overall strategic direction.

■ Establishing an Individual Invoicing Habit Until a Firm-Wide Invoicing Process Is Implemented

Since a firm-wide solution will take time to develop, Martin must still address his personal invoicing habits in the short term.

You challenge Martin's longstanding view on invoicing as a "low-value administrative work" and ask him, for example:

- How do you define "low value" versus "high value" work?
- Is all the work you currently label as "administrative" truly detrimental to your success?
- What evidence do you have for this belief?
- What counter-evidence exists?
- If a typical client overheard our conversation, how do you think they would respond?

Reflecting on these questions, Martin starts to see the value of reframing administrative work related to billing: By recognizing invoicing as an integral part of the client experience instead of a low-value administrative task, Martin can reframe invoicing as one essential component of delivering value to the client. To test this new perspective, Martin will have to send timely invoices and observe and gather relevant client feedback.

Martin also identifies two key factors—**context triggers**—that influence his invoicing behavior and can help him establish a more effective invoicing habit:

- **Timing** matters: Martin recalls that whenever he completed invoices first thing in the morning, he felt energized because he had gotten it off his chest. However, as soon as he tried to invoice late in the evening, Martin found it nearly impossible to concentrate, as his energy and willpower were already depleted by then.
- **Rewarding** the habit of invoicing: Martin also remembers that in the past—time and again—he had successfully used his negotiation skills on himself: Whenever he completed an invoice, he would immediately reward himself, for instance, setting aside an hour to work on something he truly enjoyed or treating himself to a good coffee from his favorite café.

You also ask Martin to reflect on his **learning history**:

He realizes that he learned in early life that administrative work and fun could not coexist. He remembers persistently rebelling against his father, who always insisted that unpleasant tasks had to be completed before play. As a child, he often heard his father complain that Martin was acting irresponsibly and inconsiderately toward others' needs, whether by leaving a Lego toy in the dining room, wanting to play before finishing homework, or leaving socks on the floor.

Martin now recognizes that when another partner criticizes his lack of "invoicing discipline", he is subconsciously propelled back to being that 7-year-old boy, standing in front of his annoyed father. And then, figuratively speaking, Martin refuses to pick up that stupid Lego toy.... or write the invoice, for that matter.

This newfound awareness of this formerly unconscious reaction pattern helps Martin recognize that, **today, he has a choice**. He can either react like little Martin being reprimanded by his father, or he can act in a way that best serves his change goal while also allowing him to credibly lead the significant changes he cares about within the firm.

Reflect and Act

Focus on your current situation:
- What specific conditions (e.g., time pressure, time of day, distractions, or people) make it difficult for you to act in alignment with your stated change goal?
- What conditions make it easier?

Focus on your learning history:
- When did you first have the thoughts that form your big assumption?
- How did this belief develop?
- How have your current life circumstances changed since you first adopted this assumption?
- Reflecting on your learning history and current behavior, how might you rethink your big assumption?

Transform: Change Behavior and Put Your Assumption to the Test

With your help, Martin has now gained clarity about his goal, the counterproductive behaviors that are holding him back, the hidden competing commitments that prevent him from changing his behavior, and the big assumption that fuels these competing goals—keeping him stuck.

He has already begun to reframe his big assumption, making it more flexible. Now, it is time to put the big assumption to the test:

? What will happen once Martin acts in alignment with his primary goal of regular invoicing?

Will his worst-case scenario unfold or could his new behavior result in unexpected positive outcomes?

Test Your Assumption in Real Life with Measurable Actions

Based on Martin's previous reflections, his actions will be twofold:
1. Martin initiates the development of a firm-wide invoicing process.
2. Martin establishes a more sustainable invoicing routine for himself.

Let's examine both elements.

- **Implementing a Firm-Wide Invoicing Process:**

First, having framed his big assumption to embrace a firm-wide lens, rather than focusing solely on his individual behavior, Martin discusses with partners and business services leaders how to design and pilot an automated invoicing process for the entire firm. Together, they decide to test a tool and gather feedback. Some partners will likely welcome this project, and others won't. However, most will acknowledge that Martin is stepping up to his role as Managing Partner by taking responsibility for an issue that affects the firm's performance.

▪ Testing a Personal Invoicing Routine

Second, Martin also begins to establish a more robust invoicing routine for himself, *"testing"* his big assumption while keeping risks minimal.

He commits to a simple habit-formation strategy (see also ▶ **Chap.** 9 on how to foster sustainable habits):

> As soon as I boot my computer on the last Friday of the month, I will open the invoicing table and start writing invoices. I will dedicate the first 60 minutes of the day to this task—when my energy levels are high and the office is quiet. I will immediately reward myself afterward by spending the next full hour immersed in client matters.
>
> After sending invoices, I will track clients' responses, whether they simply acknowledge receipt, or request clarifications. Additionally, I will monitor any feedback I receive from clients on the quality of my legal work to determine whether a pattern exists—as suggested by my big assumption—such as, 'the more invoicing I do, the worse the quality of my work', or whether the opposite may be true.

These small, measurable actions allow Martin to gather concrete evidence on whether—and if, to what extent—his big assumption holds up in practice.

For example, once he starts billing regularly:

- Will he really lose energy and joy in his client work?
- Will the quality of his legal work decline?
- Will clients become dissatisfied?

All of these concerns can be tested through real-world experience.

Evaluate the Results: Refine Behavior and Assumption if Needed

Like any organizational change initiative, developing a firm-wide invoicing process will be iterative. Not everything will go smoothly from day one. Martin's role will be to ensure clear communication of the why, what, and how of the changed billing process. Also, it will be essential to gather feedback on the new process, revise and adjust it, and monitor progress closely.

Martin will also evaluate the results of his personal new invoicing habit.

He might realize:

> *When I do the invoicing first thing in the morning, it doesn't drain my energy as much as I had anticipated. Rewarding myself afterward works pretty well and keeps me motivated. Clients continue to appreciate my legal work just as much as before. Some long-*

term clients have even given positive feedback about my new invoicing routine, saying it improves our professional relationship.

As a result, Martin's revised assumption might sound like this:

» *When I write invoices, I do not lose joy or energy in my client work, nor does the quality of my work decline. Clients continue to value my work and appreciate my timely invoicing as part of our professional collaboration. Besides, contrary to what I feared, I haven't lost "my excuse to avoid admin work". My COO and colleagues continue to shield me from as many administrative tasks as possible.*

Reflect and Act

- How could you test your big assumption?
- When will you do it?
- Who can support you and be a sparring partner in reflecting on the results?

Summary

10

You have now guided Martin through a process that helped him overcome personal immunity or resistance to change, which is a critical capability for personal effectiveness and for leading transformation effectively.

The immunity-to-change framework, developed by Robert Kegan and Lisa Lahey, is a powerful tool for unlocking personal transformation—both for yourself and for those you support in overcoming their own struggles to change behavior, particularly during a transformation you are leading in your firm.

That said, your conversation with Martin unfolded rather smoothly.

When you work with others to explore their struggles with behavioral transformation, patience and persistence are key to uncovering hidden psychological dynamics. High-performing colleagues who are unaccustomed to admitting awkward, embarrassing, or even painful emotions require your tactful support to acknowledge and express these feelings. In particular:
- it is essential that you remain **curious, non-judgmental, and empathetic**
- **confidentiality** is non-negotiable
- without a **solid foundation of trust**, you may not be the best sparring partner for this kind of intense, introspective work.

ACKNOWLEDGE To acknowledge underlying reasons for resistance to change behavior, you

- defined your primary goal, the desired behavior change.
- identified counterproductive behaviors.
- uncovered hidden competing goals that prevented you from changing and analyzed their rationale.

CHALLENGE To challenge the big assumption that fuels your struggles to change, you
- fleshed out your worst-case scenario and unmasked your big assumption, a deeply held, often subconscious belief that prevents you from shifting behavior.
- scrutinized the validity of this assumption and reframed it to allow for greater behavioral flexibility.

TRANSFORM To achieve sustainable behavior change, you
- put your big assumption to the test through small, measurable experiments in the real world.
- evaluated the tests' results and determined whether to further adjust behavior or big assumption to enable sustainable behavior change.

References

Kegan, R., Lahey, L., Fleming, A., & Miller, M. (2014). Making business personal. *Harvard Business Review, 92*(4), 44–52.

Kegan, R., & Lahey, L. L. (2001). The real reason people won't change. *Harvard Business Review, 79*(10), 85–92.

Kegan, R., & Lahey, L. L. (2009). *Immunity to Change: How to overcome it and unlock the potential in yourself and your organization*. Harvard Business Review Press.

Conclusion

Contents

M. Bernhardt, *Leading Transformation in Law Firms*, Law for Professionals,
https://doi.org/10.1007/978-3-031-98653-6_11

> The biggest room in the world is the room for improvement.[1]—Helmut Schmidt (German Chancellor from 1974 to 1982)

As we come to the end of this book, it is clear that **transformation is** not just an organizational challenge but **a deeply human endeavor**. Law firm leaders who succeed in navigating the complexities of transformation do so by placing people at the center of their strategies, fostering adaptability, and committing to growth, not only for their firms but also for themselves.

Throughout these pages, you have explored tools, frameworks, and stories designed to help you unlock the potential of individuals, teams, and the firm as a whole.

In a world shaped by volatility, uncertainty, complexity, and ambiguity (VUCA), the skills, mindsets, and behaviors that made us successful in the past aren't necessarily the ones that will secure success in the future. Leadership in transformative times requires you to remain curious, challenge assumptions, and adapt outdated mindsets and behaviors—both in others and in yourself.

Leadership has the power to inspire, shape culture, and lay the foundation for sustainable success. It is a responsibility that requires courage, empathy, and a deep commitment to continuous learning and reflection. Let this book serve as a companion—a foundation to build upon as you cultivate the skills and mindsets necessary to lead through the profound changes shaping the future of the legal profession.

The journey does not end here. As you reflect on what you have learned, ask yourself: *What new insights, skills, or approaches can I explore to better support individuals, teams and my firm?*

Transformation, ultimately, depends on leaders who are committed to evolving and growing continuously. As Helmut Schmidt aptly put it, there is always room to grow.

Step forward with confidence and curiosity. Continue to explore, to challenge, and to grow.

The future of your firm—and the people who make it extraordinary—lies in your hands.

Reference

Harding, L. (2015, November 10). Helmut Schmidt obituary. *The Guardian*. https://www.theguardian.com/world/2015/nov/10/helmut-schmidt

1 Harding (2015).

MIX
Papier aus verantwortungsvollen Quellen
Paper from responsible sources
FSC® C105338

If you have any concerns about our products,
you can contact us on
ProductSafety@springernature.com

In case Publisher is established outside the EU,
the EU authorized representative is:
Springer Nature Customer Service Center GmbH
Europaplatz 3, 69115 Heidelberg, Germany

Printed by Libri Plureos GmbH
in Hamburg, Germany